What Celebrities Collect!

ALSO BY MICHELE KARL

Greetings with Love: The Book of Valentines

What Celebrities Collect!

By Michele Karl
Foreword by Robin Leach

Pelican Publishing Company
Gretna 2006

*The word "Pelican" and the depiction of a pelican are trademarks
of Pelican Publishing Company, Inc., and are registered
in the U.S. Patent and Trademark Office.*

Every effort has been made to give photo credit where due. If omissions have been made, the publisher will be more than happy to add the information in future printings. All information obtained in this book was obtained through research, publicists, agents, and direct interviews with the celebrities. Values and information listed in this book were supplied as a guide. They are not intended to set prices. Neither the author nor the publisher assumes responsibility for any losses that might be incurred as a result of consulting information obtained in this book.

Library of Congress Cataloging-in-Publication Data

Karl, Michele.
  What celebrities collect! / by Michele Karl ; foreword by Robin Leach.
       p. cm.
  ISBN 1-58980-142-3 (hardcover : alk. paper)
  1. Celebrities—United States—Biography. 2. Collectors and collecting—United States—Biography. 3. United States—Social life and customs—1971- I. Title.

  AM223.K37 2004
  790.1'32'092—dc22

                                                    2003027657

Printed in Singapore

Published by Pelican Publishing Company, Inc.
1000 Burmaster Street, Gretna, Louisiana 70053

*To the love of my life, my husband, Joseph,
and my two precious angels, Mathew and Angela*

CONTENTS

Part II: Special Collector's Tribute

Part III: Celebrity-Inspired Collectibles

Just what is a fascinating book? To me, it's an informative book with which I can sit back, relax, and enjoy.

Michele Karl, a writer in the antiques and collectibles field, came up with an idea for a book that she felt would do just that, a book that would cover two of her favorite subjects: collectibles and celebrities.

After years of letters, hundreds of phone calls, and determined persistence tracking celebrities and interviewing them about their collections, she has been able to garner what is before you now: *What Celebrities Collect!* This book shows a side of celebrities no one has really seen before. The effort she has put into this project is evident in the information and enjoyment that you will now be able to share. It is a project long overdue. It is a unique and different opportunity to see into the private lives of some very public and not-so-public people, including myself, with my collection of marine paperweights.

Hosting *Lifestyles of the Rich and Famous* for nearly fifteen years gave me the opportunity to travel to many exotic places visiting celebrities. From dinners with Roger Moore, overlooking the Mediterranean in the south of France, to meeting Ivana Trump at Le Cirque in New York, I've logged more than a million miles and have traveled to every country in the world, except two! Those travels permitted me to acquire some of the most beautiful paperweights imaginable.

While at my home on Jumby Bay in Antigua in the Caribbean, I am able to see an abundance of beautiful sea life. Collecting marine paperweights and keeping them with me in America gives me the opportunity to still feel "at home" while working on my many projects. Every time I need to think about the blue, tranquil waters of my home, I simply gaze into one of my hundred-plus paperweights and feel as if I were there.

Michele Karl's book *What Celebrities Collect!* gives you the opportunity to see fascinating and various collections of many of the same celebrities whom I have had the pleasure of interviewing throughout my career. I hope you'll get the same sense of meeting the stars and seeing a little of their private lives as you view this extraordinary book.

Collecting is something that has brought me great pleasure. Whether the collector is you, a friend, or a family member, the act of collecting is something that can be shared, as many of the celebrities in this book do by sharing their collections with you.

So settle back with a glass of your favorite bubbly and enjoy this in-depth, entertaining book. Champagne wishes.

ROBIN LEACH

ACKNOWLEDGMENTS

Putting a book like this together takes years of research as well as help from others, with their ideas, leads, and encouragement. I'd like to thank the following people for their support and inspiration during this project: Elisa Agostinho, Kathy Bartels, Dennis and Marlene Grant, Ralph Merlino, Ken and Sunnie Newell, Kenneth Lee Newell, Rob Heroux, Shooting Stars Photography, and JSK Photography; to Robin Leach for writing the foreword and being the first to respond when I started this project several years ago; to Angie Holmann for her help in proofing; to Pelican Publishing for taking on this project, Nina Kooij, and Stephanie Williams (for her constant encouragement); and to many of my Internet friends for their help with images. Last, but not least, I'd like to say thank you to the many celebrities, their publicists, and agents who participated in this project, making it such a wonderful book! Thank you!

A few years back, I thought of a wonderful idea for a book. As a writer in the antiques and collectibles field, and with my latest book in stores, it was time for my next adventure. What would the public be interested in reading?

I've always been interested in antiques and collectibles, with an equally strong engrossment in another area: celebrities. How about a book on what celebrities collect? What a great idea! After checking several avenues as to whether there was indeed interest in such a book, I quickly determined that it was time to embark on my next great adventure: *What Celebrities Collect!* The response from everyone was overwhelming.

Next came the hard part: tracking down the celebrity collectors and obtaining their participation. Seeing the amount of investigating, interviewing, and assembling that would need to be done to gather what valuable information such a project would require, I realized this was to be a time-consuming endeavor.

I checked my answering machine, e-mail, and mailbox daily until it finally produced the very first response from my initial attempts at reaching the celebrity collectors. It was from one of my favorite celebrities: Robin Leach.

How exciting to get his letter, along with a gorgeous photograph of him with his collection of marine paperweights! I'll never forget that moment.

Now, nearly six years later—and after relentlessly contacting everyone from celebrities, to agents, to publicists (some of whom now recognize my voice when they answer the phone)—my efforts have brought personal interviews or correspondence from over one hundred celebrity collectors.

While some celebrities were busy filming movies or on concert tour when contacted, many of their agents and publicists made sure I had clippings and information to include their clients in this project. To them, I say thank you!

To hear what is in the minds and hearts of so many famous people has truly been an interesting journey, a journey that you, the reader, will be able to take as you follow an adventurous tour of hobbies, obsessions, and loves to the hearts and souls of your favorite celebrities.

What Celebrities Collect! is the result of many years of serious effort, an effort that was worth every minute. And once you read through this interesting book, you'll see why. I hope you enjoy reading it as much as I've enjoyed writing it.

Happy Collecting!

MICHELE KARL

Dan Aykroyd likes to wear all types of hats—actor, comedian, director, television writer, and screenwriter—and he's good at all of them.

A Canadian, Aykroyd came into the living rooms of Americans with the smash television hit *Saturday Night Live* when it debuted in 1975. After five years of playing everyone from Richard Nixon to Julia Child on the series, he would move on to movies, taking his *Saturday Night Live* "Blues Brother" and long-time friend, John Belushi, along with him. *The Blues Brothers* was Aykroyd's first movie, and he wrote the screenplay. Other movies followed, including *Doctor Detroit, Trading Places, Ghostbusters, Spies Like Us,* and *Dragnet.* He received his first Best Supporting Actor nomination for his performance in *Driving Miss Daisy.*

This Blues Brother likes more than just playing a ghostbuster. One of his hobbies includes reading about the supernatural. This is where he got the idea for *Ghostbusters.*

Aykroyd has an extensive collection of books on the supernatural. He enjoys ufology—the study of UFOs (unidentified flying objects). He was quoted in *Private Clubs* as saying, "But I am also interested in those who've gone before and in spirits that linger because they haven't been satisfied in this life. My great-grandfather was an Edwardian spiritualist who belonged to the British Society for Psychical Research, and he got the entire family thinking along these lines back three generations ago. My grandfather had séances in the farmhouse. My father read everything he could on trance mediumship, where the medium will go into a trance and become another person, speak in another voice. They did a lot of that. So this stuff was lying around the house, and it was natural for me to have an interest in it."

Besides reading about ghosts and goblins, Aykroyd is said to be a bit of a law-enforcement buff and, thus, collects badges. I've heard that

he's even been known to do an occasional ride-along in a squad car!

Though not confirmed, rumors around toy shows say that Aykroyd has a fondness for a little twelve-inch guy named GI Joe. He is a great actor, writer, and director and a dedicated collector as well.

JUICY TIDBIT!

Aykroyd isn't the only one who believes in ghosts. Actresses Greta Garbo, Marilyn Monroe, and Lucille Ball all sought out a clairvoyant, according to a story in *McCalls.* Even Princess Diana met with a British medium named Rita Rogers. According to the same story in *McCalls,* Barbra Streisand and Madonna have also had consultations with psychics. Aykroyd told *McCalls,* in a fall 1999 interview, that he was convinced that spirits not only existed but also were dwelling in his Canadian home. He had heard a strange knocking ("a kind of electronic snap") when no one else was present, and he had seen lights flickering on and off by themselves. He stated, "The house has a history of spiritual activity that would blow your mind."

Dan Aykroyd *(AP Photo)*

An example of a scary book Aykroyd could collect.

Do you know which musical instrument actor Matthew Broderick collects?

a) Guitars
b) Trombones
c) Flutes

According to representatives from the History Channel, the answer is trombones.

I've heard Matthew and his wife, Sarah Jessica Parker, also collect illy cups. These delicate coffee cups are made in limited edition and created by international artists. The coffee cup and plate are signed and numbered and run about thirty dollars each. Another collector who is said to collect the interesting sets is Francis Ford Coppola.

DID YOU KNOW?

Music buff and talk-show host Bill Maher has an extensive music library. Included in his collection are shelves of old vinyl albums and forty-fives and hundreds of CDs. They are sorted by decade and genre. Maher told *People*, "I don't collect art or cars or motorcycles. I'm a file guy." Evidently, that's true. According to the article, his home office contains twenty-two separate file drawers, each filled with carefully labeled folders.

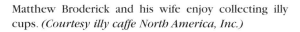

Matthew Broderick and his wife enjoy collecting illy cups. *(Courtesy illy caffe North America, Inc.)*

Matthew Broderick and his wife, Sarah Jessica Parker. *(AP Photo)*

Nicolas Cage, an actor, director, and producer, has a love for comic books, which he started collecting as a child. He even acquired the double-print image of Superman that artist Andy Warhol designed, extending his love of comics to the form of fine art. This love brought him his stage name of Nicolas Cage, after comic-book character Luke Cage *(Hero for Hire)*. Growing up, Cage staged scenes for shows and spent hours imagining himself as a comic-book character. Nicolas told *Movieline,* "Comic books and cartoons have a lot of influence in my life. I'm like a sponge. I could see a commercial on TV and get an idea, just the delivery someone gave will stay in my head, and I will spew it back out."

Cage parted with his favorites when Heritage Comics of Dallas auctioned his comic collection of 141 lots for $1.68 million. Among the highlights of Nicolas Cage's collection was a 1940 Detective #38 comic that featured the debut of Batman's sidekick, Robin, the Boy Wonder. It went for $120,750, over a price-guide list of $45,000. A 1940 All-Star Comic #3, introducing the Justice Society of America, sold for an amazing $126,500, against a value of $45,000. It was the first comic book to introduce a superhero team. The Justice Society of America included characters like the Green Lantern, the Flash, Hawkman, Hourman, Dr. Fate, the Spectre, the Sandman, and the Atom. Cage's comic book marking the first appearance of Superman (Action Comics #1 from 1938) sold for $86,250, including buyer's premium.

With a total of $5.2 million, the sale, which also included comic art, movie posters, and memorabilia not in Nicolas Cage's collection, set a new world record for comic-book auctions.

Besides comic books and superheroes, Cage has a passion for sports cars. He plays the role of movie star well by driving not one, but a variety of European sports cars from his collection. It's been said that he has paid as much as half a million dollars for a car to indulge his collecting habit. Cage's collection of automobiles consists of many types and models, including an Austin-Healey that gave him a scare on the freeway by spinning out of control one night. His collection is composed of Corvette Stingrays (namely a 1967 metallic-blue version nicknamed the Blue Shark), Lamborghinis, Bentleys, Ferraris, and a 1967 Chevelle, to mention a few. One of the rarest cars in Cage's assortment is a 1971 Lamborghini Miura SVJ, once owned by the late Shah of Iran. The car, which was auctioned off at a Geneva, Switzerland, auction house, sold for nearly double the preestimate value, at $446,820. It's a metallic-burgundy beauty, the first of only four SVJs built, and was in mint condition when purchased by Cage. The speedometer read less than two thousand miles. Cage became the proud owner of the Lamborghini in 1997. At its selling price, it was the most expensive car auctioned off in Europe that year.

Though Cage also loves writing short stories and screenplays, he has said that if he wasn't acting he'd probably be designing cars or starting a comic-book company.

I hope he isn't reading his comics while driving one of his sports cars!

Top: Nicolas Cage *(Courtesy Shooting Stars)*

The Adventures of Superman, Showcase, and Ghost Rider comic books. *(Photographs of copyrighted D.C. Comics and Marvel Comics comic-book covers)*

This singer/musician uses his collection of guitars for a good cause. The West Indies rehab center on the island of Antigua, Crossroads Centre, which Eric Clapton helps fund, was causing a financial drain on the guitarist. The center was anticipating rich patients from overseas. Instead, the local residents are taking advantage of the free medical care the center offers at Clapton's expense. Therefore, Clapton auctioned off a portion of his guitar collection to help the center. The auction was held in 1999 at Christie's Auction House. In all, Clapton auctioned off one hundred stage and studio guitars, including "Brownie," the famous 1956 Fender Stratocaster he used for the *Layla* sessions; a rare 1958 Gibson Explorer; a 1974 Martin 000-28 steel string; a 1959 Gibson ES-335; a 1952 Fender Telecaster; and a 1956 Gibson ES-350TN. "Brownie" alone was expected to fetch $80,000 to $100,000. A 1954 Fender Stratocaster sold to Michael Malone of AEI Music for $211,500. Two lots were purchased by actor Michael J. Fox via telephone, including a 1949 Gibson-125 for $36,800 and a circa-1930s National Duolian for $42,500. Expected to garner over $1 million, the auction ultimately raised over $5 million.

The top sales were "Brownie" (used on the whole *Layla* album), which sold for $497,500, and a 1954 Fender Stratocaster (used in the mid-1970s for slide, stage, and recording), which sold for $211,500. Clapton said the idea of auctioning off the guitars came from the Crossroads Centre's fundraising committee.

Some collections are put to good use, as was this one.

Hamish Dodds, president and CEO of the Hard Rock Café, secured over $250,000 in Eric Clapton memorabilia, including guitars and a purple Versace suit worn by Clapton, to adorn the walls of cafés around the world. *(AP Photo)*

Top: Eric Clapton *(AP Photo)*

It's no secret that Dick Clark loves rock-'n'-roll. Known as the "World's Oldest Teenager," Clark has built an empire out of the music. His restaurants, under the name Dick Clark's American Bandstand Grille, house a large amount of the rock-'n'-roll memorabilia he has collected over the years. When *Bandstand* was picked up by ABC in 1957, Clark changed its name to *American Bandstand*, ended the shows "all-white policy," and began introducing black artists. By 1959, it was broadcast by 101 affiliates and reached an audience of twenty million.

Clark was inducted into the Radio Hall of Fame in 1990 and the Rock and Roll Hall of Fame in 1993. Clark, of Dick Clark Productions, is much more than a great businessman. He is an avid collector with years in the entertainment business, giving him easy access to an

Dick Clark *(Courtesy Dick Clark)*

array of great collectibles. I've been told that his office is full of show-biz memorabilia, with items that include Bo Diddley's boots and a cape owned by the one-and-only Elvis Presley.

Since his collection is so large, the restaurants are a perfect place to display his memorabilia. Having them for show in the restaurants also gives other collectors an opportunity to view this awe-inspiring assortment of items. The restaurants, located in the Indianapolis and Newark International Airports, cover their walls with vintage photos, gold records, artists' contracts, and rare posters, among other things. All of the items shown in the restaurant are part of Clark's personal collection. Clark has spent a lifetime collecting a lifetime of memories.

American Bandstand Grill *(Courtesy Dick Clark)*

Academy Award-winning actor and heart-throb George Clooney, who played Dr. Doug Ross on the hit television series *ER* and starred in several great films, can be seen driving around the streets of L.A. on one of his favorite motorcycles. The star, who played Batman in the film *Batman & Robin,* has no trouble holding up the two-wheeled machines. Harleys are certainly a favorite. He's even been known to buy motorcycles for friends.

In an interview with Riccardo Romani, Clooney talked about his first bike: "It was a Harley, like those in endowment to the police. It was 1982. Then I got a Honda-like chopper. Recently, I have exaggerated. I've bought five in only one go, for my friends, for going around all together. But the new Indian bikes aren't good enough. They give you a lot of problems. The old ones were better. I've had one [from the year] 1949, a spectacle." Clooney works on the bikes himself when they need a little work. In that same interview, Clooney stated, "It's the most funny part. I want to say, I have taken two hours and I have gotten dirty up to the ears, but you don't know what satisfaction it is when the motorbike runs again. Whoever loves the motorbike knows about it, there is no need to explain it. This is the reason for which I prefer the old motorbikes to those new ones. Perhaps it is a romantic thing, but those new bikes always leave you afoot and stop. You cannot do anything."

Always the nice guy, Clooney helped donate several BMW C1 scooters equipped with first-aid equipment to the Italian people so others can ride around and help people at the same time!

Now let's just hope George wears his helmet. I'd hate to see that pretty face all scratched up.

George Clooney *(AP Photo)*

George Clooney stands in Rome's Campidoglio square next to one of the ten BMW C1 scooters equipped with first aid for heart problems donated by Clooney, Italian pop singer Lucio Dalla, and the Running Heart Foundation. *(AP Photo)*

Bringing sounds of Frank Sinatra into this generation, the swing and big-band music of crooner Harry Connick, Jr. would leave any woman falling over her table to get closer to this New Orleans dream man. Growing up in New Orleans with a love for jazz, Connick would wear suits. Now living in Connecticut with his wife, Victoria's Secret model Jill Goodacre, and their children, Connick takes every opportunity to dress his best. Today his Gucci suits are the top of fashion, but they are never topped off with one of the pairs of cuff links from his collection. He talked to *InStyle* about his cuff-link collection and said,

"I never, never wear them. I don't know why I collect them. My Aunt Lil in California sent me some that were my uncle's. They're costume jewelry. I have a case my wife gave me that sits on my dresser; it's full of unused cuff links." Perhaps some day Connick will put his collection to good use by wearing some of his different pieces. Did I mention that besides being a collector, Connick is also a great guy? He brought my daughter, Angela, on stage and sang her a song while performing in Knoxville. Angela now has a Harry Connick, Jr. autographed collectible teddy bear to remember the occasion.

Harry Connick, Jr. *(AP Photo)*

Cuff links are Connick's collection of choice.

The hunt is on, and Norm Crosby is out for the capture. When asked what he collected, Crosby said, "Social Security!" Leave it to this great comedian to come back with a quick joke. But thirty-five years of collecting elephants is no laughing matter for this collector.

"My wife, Joan, collects elephants, and so whenever I travel, I am always on the lookout for unique models of elephants," states Crosby. For the Crosbys, collecting is a family tradition. Joan's family has been collecting elephants for three generations. Crosby says, "There are elephants made of wood, bronze, Lalique, silver, glass, plaster, pewter, etc." The list can go on forever. The selection is as enormous as the elephant's trunk! Lalique, silver, and bronze versions can be quite expensive, while ones made of wood, plaster, and other materials can run much lower in cost.

"My favorites are the smallest ones, because they are easy to carry in my shoulder bag!" Big or small, the important thing is that the elephant has its trunk up. According to Crosby, "Only elephants with their trunks raised are considered collectible." Crosby points out that an important thing to remember about collecting elephants with the trunks raised is that they are said to bring good luck. The elephants should have their trunks facing into the house to bring in the good luck. With all the groupings in this collector's home, he is sure to have enough luck to last a lifetime.

Crosby is always looking for new pieces to add to his and his wife's collection. He told *Collectibles Illustrated,* "Searching for elephants gives you something to do when you're away from home. When I go places where I've been several times and there are no interesting things to do, I can always go to the antique shops or other stores and look for elephants." He continued, "I was working at a nightclub in Washington, DC one time and got to know everyone at a particular hotel where I stayed. One day the cashier in the coffee shop said she had something to give me. It turned out to be a little gold elephant. She told me that several years before, she had been a hotel clerk at the front desk in one of the big Washington hotels and that Bob Hope—whose good luck charm was an elephant—came in and gave it to her for good luck. She said, 'I want to give it to you so that it will bring you the same luck that Bob Hope had.' I took it and put it in my tuxedo pocket. This was in the late '50s. And, believe it or not, I have never done a show of any sort to this day that I don't have that little elephant in my pocket. I've even held up a show that was about to start so that I could go all the way back up to my room and get my little elephant."

Norm Crosby and his elephant collection. *(Courtesy Ralph Merlino)*

Whether as a city slicker or an Oscar host, Billy Crystal can keep you in stitches with his unique brand of humor. Billed as one of America's favorite masters of ceremonies, he can look you in the eye and, with an expression or gesture, put a smile on your face. The star of such movies as *When Harry Met Sally, My Giant,* and *City Slickers,* Crystal has also starred on television, in the weekly hit *Soap,* and has been a regular at the Comic Relief benefit shows, along with fellow collectors Whoopi Goldberg and Robin Williams.

A devoted Yankees fan, Crystal's collecting passions run to the old-fashioned or "take me out to the ball game" days, with baseball and sporting memorabilia hitting a home run. Keeping him away from baseball is not an easy thing to do. In an interview with Yahoo, Crystal stated, "I was making *My Giant* in the middle of the Czech Republic during baseball season. Each day I would call up ESPN and other sports sites to get scores." Crystal has even gone so far as to purchase a small percentage of a baseball team, the Arizona Diamondbacks.

He loves baseball so much he's stated that if he wasn't acting or being a comedian he'd be playing the game. With Crystal's love of baseball has come the love of collecting sports memorabilia. In the same interview, he stated, "I have mostly Mickey Mantle stuff. I was given an award by the Anti-Defamation League in New York. Instead of a plaque, they gave me an original chair from Yankee Stadium. Mickey signed it: 'Dear Billy, I wish I was still playing and you were still sitting here.' He's the guy who made me want to play baseball. I love the game."

Though he has no regrets for not playing baseball, the thought of how far he could have gone does enter his mind. Crystal can think about baseball while at his office, Face Productions, in Beverly Hills, based within the larger headquarters of his pal Rob Reiner's Castle Rock Entertainment office. His office is decorated with animal prints, antiques, and his collection of baseball and sports memorabilia. The walls and most available spaces are taken with framed movie posters, vintage pictures of Mickey Mantle, and collectibles. Some of Crystal's pieces include a boxing glove signed by Muhammad Ali; basketballs given to him by friends, including Michael Jordan; and a bat given to him by Mickey Mantle's family. Crystal told *InStyle* magazine, "Baseball is my thing. I called myself Mickey in *Forget Paris,* and I've mentioned him [Mickey Mantle] in a lot of movies. When Mickey died, Bob Costas called and said, 'You gotta come [to the funeral]. Do you want to speak?' I said no, but we stayed up till 4 A.M. writing the eulogy—which Bob delivered—like two college kids cramming for an exam."

Crystal continued, "I sat in George Steinbrenner's box with Joe DiMaggio and Henry Kissinger, whom I'd met before on the Concorde. He said, 'I want to say something: You look mahvelous!'" It was then that Crystal picked up yet another souvenir, a cigar from the 1996 World Series.

Crystal's favorite baseball player, Mickey Mantle, is a favorite of many. It has been reported that Crystal bought a 1956 Mickey Mantle glove for $239,000 at Sotheby's auction. The glove formerly belonged to Barry Halper, a well-known sports-memorabilia collector. Halper told *Trade Fax,* "He's [Crystal] going to play with it. He wants a good workout using Mickey's glove."

Top: Billy Crystal *(Courtesy Shooting Stars)*

Mickey Mantle's baseball glove, which is now in Crystal's collection.

When I first met actress and children's-book author Jamie Lee Curtis in Chicago, I told her that I had heard she collected photographs. She seemed surprised that I knew but was happy to confirm that she does. "Yes, I do collect photographs, mainly black-and-white photos," she said. "I tried to collect some of the master contemporary photographers."

While Curtis's father, Tony, is an accomplished painter (her mother was actress Janet Leigh), it's the black-and-white photographs this amateur photographer loves. She said she had been collecting them for "quite some time" and that many of the photos in her collection are very emotional for her.

Curtis told Homestore.com, "I love very poignant black-and-white photos. One of my favorites is of a woman obviously poor and troubled. I don't know how I identified with the anguish the woman in the photo is going through, but there is something so evocative about the picture that it continues to affect me. Photographs do that to me—paintings, not as much. There are certain photographs that can wipe me out. I take pictures so I'm much more into photography than anything else."

Besides photographs, Curtis has kept some slates from various movies in which she has appeared, including *True Lies, Halloween, Blue Steel, A Fish Called Wanda*, and *Perfect*.

Jamie Lee Curtis *(AP Photo)*

Jamie Lee loves photography like this black-and-white photograph by Dorothea Lange. *(Library of Congress)*

Cartoonist Jim Davis has a constant companion. He's a fat, lazy, wisecracking, lasagna-eating cat named Garfield. Davis created Garfield in 1978 and since then the phenomenal success of that little cat has done nothing but grow. GARFIELD® is the most widely syndicated Sunday comic in the United States and worldwide has more than 220 million readers daily. The "Garfield" books have been translated into twenty-six languages. Garfield had his own series on CBS television and countless prime-time specials, and a plethora of "Garfield" merchandise sells in sixty-nine countries.

Davis's love (besides Garfield, of course) is wines, however, not just any wine. Davis prefers to collect and buy wines by vintage. He told me, "Prices of old wines at auctions have gone crazy. One of the most valuable collections belongs to Hardy Rodenstock, a German music publisher, who owns eighteenth-century wines that belonged to Jefferson." *Forbes* magazine bought one of the bottles, a Chateau Lafite 1787, in 1985 for a record price of $156,450. That is $22,350 a glass. According to Jancis Robinson, author and wine expert (from an interview with *Parade*), "They kept it in a museum and it spoiled under a spotlight. Thus the world's most expensive wine became the world's most expensive vinegar." Davis said, "I have a few thousand bottles of wine in my collection." He also collects limited-edition books as well as "Garfield" memorabilia.

He also wanted me to share with everyone that Garfield isn't a collector, but Jon is. "He collects socks," said Davis. "He has a sock drawer and sorts them by color and style."

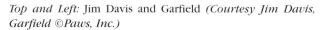

Top and Left: Jim Davis and Garfield *(Courtesy Jim Davis, Garfield ©Paws, Inc.)*

Right: Jim Davis with his wine collection. *(Courtesy Jim Davis, Garfield ©Paws, Inc.)*

One of my favorite actors, Johnny Depp, has starred in a multitude of films after his humble beginning on the television series *21 Jump Street*, including movies like *A Nightmare on Elm Street, Edward Scissorhands,* and *Pirates of the Caribbean.* The star, who bought Bela Lugosi's old mansion in the Hollywood Hills, is also a musician who plays the guitar. Depp has played in over fifteen different bands.

This actor has several collections. A big fan of author Jack Kerouac, the American writer known for such books as *On the Road* and *Big Sur,* Depp has framed letters by the author hanging in his home and collects first-edition copies of his books. Depp would love to star in a movie based on the author's work (screenwriters get busy). In an interview with *Movieline,* Depp talked about the book *On the Road,* stating, "I thought I'd buy the rights, then thought I'd be doing an injustice to the real thing. Kerouac had to write those books. Most movies only get made because a company thinks it's a good idea, financially." An article in *Rolling Stone* stated that Depp's prized possession, and one that cost him a good portion of his burgeoning fortune, is a book on black culture in whose margins Kerouac has scribbled and doodled. According to Depp, "It's a piece of history. I look at it everyday." Depp also owns several items that once belonged to Kerouac, including two jackets, a raincoat, a suitcase, some correspondence, and, of course, original manuscripts. Depp even went as far as meeting Kerouac's in-laws.

Depp has another collection that some may find a bit strange. A March 1997 *Newsweek* article states, "Depp loves bugs. He collects them, mounted old style with pins in glass boxes." His favorite bug store is in Paris. As a child, Depp loved bugs, especially the

Rare books similar to those that Depp collects.

Top: Johnny Depp *(Courtesy Shooting Stars)*

bugs and lizards he encountered living in Florida. In an interview with the actor, *GQ* stated that his home is "carpeted with books and CD's and ashtrays; heaps of eccentric collectibles (bats and bugs, a pigeon skeleton and paintings of clowns); photographs of his heroes William Burroughs and Jack Kerouac and his family; the hat and cane from *Benny & Joon* and that *Scissorhands* piece hanging on the wall." According to a story in *Biography,* mass murderer John Wayne Gacy painted one of the scary clown paintings Depp once owned.

Other items the actor has in his collection include: a souvenir from *Edward Scissorhands,* the bladed limbs and a prototype for an Edward Scissorhands doll that never got made, the wig for his part in *Fear and Loathing in Las Vegas,* and a "Wanted" poster from *Dead Man.* Depp likes to keep items from the various movies in which he has appeared. In an interview with *Vogue,* Depp stated, "I keep stuff from movies so I can give it to my grandchildren someday...if I have them."

In that same interview, it's stated that Depp has oddly shaped arts-and-craft lamps to go along with his collection of art-deco furnishings, black-and-white photographs, and gilt-framed seventeenth-century Italian oil paintings he bought in Paris. He also owned a personalized record plaque from Oasis and pictures of Jean Cocteau.

Depp is the kind of collector who transforms his collecting passions as often as he changes roles. Who knows what may strike this actor's fancy in the future?

Celine Dion is an incredible singer who has sold over 50 million albums worldwide, picking up Grammy Awards along the way. At age twelve, her recording (a song written by her mother) ended up in the hands of Quebec music entrepreneur René Angélil (now her husband and manager), and the rest, you can say, is history.

Some people's collections can almost be called an obsession that goes to their heads. For Dion, it goes right to her feet. The diva with the golden voice, who placed on *Forbes'* list of top-paid celebrities, has a soft spot for fashion and shoes. She prefers couture clothing ranging in prices from a few thousand dollars to ten thousand dollars apiece, and her shoes reflect the elegance of her dresses. Dion's collection is said to be anywhere from five hundred to one thousand pairs of shoes. If she finds a style of shoe she likes, she will buy it in different colors. Many of the styles are high heeled and come from such makers as Manolo Blahnik, Prada, and Valentino. The price on the designer versions can run anywhere from five hundred to one thousand dollars.

In an article for *Ladies Home Journal,* Celine's stage-outfit stylist and frequent shopping companion stated, "She is not a snob about anything." Montreal designer Annie Horth stated in the same interview that Dion loves everything from Nike footwear to Diesel jeans. "We pass in front of Club Monaco or Banana Republic and something in the window catches her eye and she's like, 'Okay, let's go!' Whether it's $2,000.00 or $29.99, she likes it or she doesn't."

Her beginnings were much more humble, with her father supporting fourteen children while her mother was a homemaker. Coming from a poor family, Celine has grown to appreciate her financial gains by sharing openly with her siblings and giving them thousands of dollars a year. Growing from a little girl with one pair of shoes to an American diva with hundreds of pairs in her possession is almost like winning the lottery. Dion's ten-million-dollar nine-bedroom vacation home in Juniper, Florida, has plenty of space to store her collection, and with sales in one year racking up to more than $55 million dollars, she has the money to spend on them. Their Florida home was the first home that she and husband René had built together and boasts a luxurious master-bedroom suite with a three-hundred-square-foot closet and motorized shelves to hold part of her wonderful shoe collection. The cost to build was reportedly around two hundred thousand dollars. The closet was built with marble floors and antique furniture. Having a home with a size of over eighteen thousand square feet, not to mention her home in Montreal, Dion will have lots of room to store any additional purchases and keep her feet very happy at the same time.

While trying on her shoes, Dion can always watch television. I've been told that her home has thirty-three television sets. Dion's other obsession? Golf. She is known to play it whenever she gets a free moment. Perhaps she will take up a collection of golf memorabilia. Who knows?

Top: Celine Dion *(AP Photo)*

Bottom: Celine Dion is truly fond of shoes.

There are many words used to describe Patty Duke, including Academy Award-winning actress, author, mother, wife, animal lover, and, last but not least, collector!

So what puts a smile on this Academy Award winner's face? Collecting Beanie Babies! Duke is the proud owner of over 160 Beanies. She collects them along with her youngest son, Kevin, from their one-hundred-acre ranch home in Idaho.

Duke tells about how she began collecting: "Beanie Babies were out for a long time before I ever knew they existed. Collecting them really came about as an accident. My plane was delayed and I was at the airport looking around and there were these Beanie Babies in the airport stores. I thought, 'Oh, these [are] those Beanie Babies everyone is talking about.' So I bought five of them to bring home to my son Kevin. Four of the bears and one named Ears the bunny. They were awfully cute."

Duke's favorites now include Beak the bird and any of the bears. States Duke, "I remember with great excitement getting my first Canadian one. I was working in Canada at the time. It was an expensive Beanie Baby but I decided to indulge and buy him. That bear was followed by the American Flag bear and Glory. It was really a big deal when we got Glory. It's funny but my husband, Michael, and I get just as excited as Kevin does when we get new ones."

So where does Duke find most of her Beanies? "We find them in different places. Being Irish, the last place you'd find me is in a pawnshop. I had never been in a pawnshop in my life. Well, now we have worn a path to the door! The pawnshops save the Beanies for us. We also get them from gift shops. The local stores are good about giving us a call when new ones come in."

Reflecting on her collecting experience, Patty says, "Typically, I have never been a collector. One year I collected watches; another year it was this or that but I never really stuck with one thing until the Beanies. I've been collecting them the longest. It's Eagle Eye Time!"

Duke and her family have plenty of room to store Beanies on their ranch, filled with an array of real-life animals, including dogs, cats, goats, horses, and birds. But they decided to keep the collection in one place. "Since they are a collection, we decided to keep them together. Kevin's bedroom walls are covered with white shelves all filled with Beanies." Duke adds, "Kevin and I will continue to collect Beanies. We don't buy them with the intent to someday sell them; we buy what we like. That is what makes them so special."

Besides Beanie Babies, Duke has a large collection of pillboxes. "My fans send them to me. I have several different types made out of enamel and porcelain. It's an enormous collection. I began collecting [them] because a lifelong medication was prescribed to me. I didn't like the stigma of taking it everyday so I decided to make it pretty. That was the beginning. The first one I bought myself and then the word got out. People have given me some of the most exquisite boxes and I use them. I use about five of them every day and then I rotate. After a few months, I'll switch to some others. I must have a couple of hundred of them. People are very generous. My husband gave me quite a few as well."

Duke also has a doll collection that came from her mother. "She would give me a doll a year," said Duke. "Each year she would say, 'This is going to be your last doll so take care of it.' I still have all the dolls she gave me." Duke admits to having a few other collections. "I also collect angels, antique clocks, candleholders, John Deere miniatures, pocket watches, silver spoons, vintage linens, and teddy bears, to name a few items."

Top: Patty Duke *(AP Photo)*

Bottom: Pillboxes like those that Patty Duke may collect.

If you could make any postage stamp you wanted, what would it be like? That was the question posed to Hallie Eisenberg. Her answer: "I'd want it to look like a Beanie Baby! I would want to put in as many Beanie Babies that could fit in the picture." She obviously is a true Beanie Baby fan!

Eisenberg is the girl with the cute dimples and the deep voice who starred in the popular Pepsi television commercials. Since then she has gone on to star in several feature films. Like most girls, Eisenberg likes playing with her friends, listening to music, and collecting Beanie Babies.

Beginning an acting career at the age of four, Eisenberg was cast to star in the movie *Paulie* after an agent discovered her at one of her sibling's auditions. Since her debut, she has rubbed shoulders with some of the best leading actors in Hollywood, including Al Pacino, Minnie Driver, and her costar in the movie *Bicentennial Man,* Robin Williams. Eisenberg said, "Al Pacino is exactly like Robin Williams. They are both *so funny!*" She has also worked alongside actress and author Jamie Lee Curtis. "Jamie gave me all of the children's books she has written. She is really nice, and I really like her books."

The New Jersey native began collecting Beanies at the tender age of two. "I got my first Beanie Baby then. It was Bongo, the monkey, and my mother gave it to me. I'm not sure how many I have now but I think it's around 107. I like to play with them with my friends. I just love them! We play with them all the time."

Eisenberg says that all of her friends collect Beanie Babies. "We play with them even if we have the same ones. We pretend that they are twins!" Besides Bongo, Goatie is another favorite. "I like them because they are *so cute!*"

Her mother, Amy, stated, "Hallie has one of the most extensive collections in the neighborhood." Even her dog, Simone, a Maltese-poodle, loves her Beanies. "My dog plays with the dog Beanie. I try to get my cat to play with my Beanies, but she is thirteen years old and she just lays on my couch."

Eisenberg describes her love of Beanies this way: "Beanies are fun and good to have. Everyone loves them. They are just like a different animal. I think Beanie Babies are better than regular stuffed animals because they are so much softer."

A big music fan, she was excited to hear that there was a set of the Spice Girls Beanies and soon added them to her collection, which consists mainly of Ty Beanies and ones she bought with her mother from a street vendor in California.

Beanies fill Eisenberg's home. "I have them upstairs and downstairs. They are all over my house, but most of them are in a big, humongous box that's in my bedroom." She also has several of the McDonald's Teenie Beanie Babies. States mother Amy, "We did the drive-through every day when the McDonald's Teenie Beanies came out."

Asked what Eisenberg plans to do with her Beanies when she grows up, she responded, "I'm going to keep them and give some to my children." And what about her future plans? "I plan to keep on acting and I'm going to keep collecting Beanie Babies!"

One of Hallie's prized Beanies is Millennium. She received it as part of a cast gift from director Chris Columbus while filming *Bicentennial Man.* When Eisenberg arrived at her trailer the day of shooting, she was greeted with a boxful of a dozen Beanie Babies, including Erin and Millennium, which she had been wanting. Chris has four children of his own, and according to Amy, he knew just which ones to get. It appears Beanies have truly gone Hollywood!

An accomplished actor and a rising star in Hollywood, Eisenberg, while a little older than when she first started collecting, cherishes her collection. Can't you just picture this cute girl—with long dark curls, a big smile, and sparkling eyes—with her Beanies? "I'm going to keep my Beanies forever."

Top: Hallie Eisenberg *(Courtesy Amy Eisenberg)*

Bottom: Hallie with her Beanie Babies. *(Courtesy Amy Eisenberg)*

Elvira (Cassandra Peterson) told me that one of the most unique gifts she received to add to her collection of gothic items was a bat skeleton, given to her by actor Nicolas Cage. Elvira has been collecting gothic-type items for years. She started when she created her character Elvira. "Pieces come from all different places," stated Elvira. "I just love collecting."

Elvira said she also collects art, especially by an illustrator named Olivia (Olivia DeBerardinis) who does illustrations for *Playboy* magazine. "Olivia drew a picture of me once," said Elvira. "It's a picture of me with Pomeranians all over the place." But gothic items are by far her favorite.

DID YOU KNOW?

Talk-show host Howard Stern is a comic-book collector, or so fellow collector and toy mogul (Spawn action figures and others) Todd MacFarlane says. Somehow, this form of collecting seems right for Stern. I can definitely picture him sitting back and reading them.

Top: Elvira ©2004 Queen "B" Productions, Inc. Used by permission ("Elvira" and "Mistress of the Dark" are registered trademarks and the exclusive property of Queen "B" Productions, Inc. Used by permission.)

Bottom: A number of Elvira's Gothic mementos.

From being princess to spokesperson, Princess Fergie plays no games and says what she thinks. She has a great personality and reflects that when you talk to her.

"I collect Wedgwood," Ferguson told me when we met in Tampa, Florida, where Ferguson was promoting the china. "I carry around a tea set with me wherever I go, and I have several older pieces that have been passed down in my family."

Wedgwood is a British maker of fine china that has been around for nearly three centuries. The company was established in 1759 in Staffordshire, England, by Josiah Wedgwood and is still based in the Midlands region of Britain, where eleven generations of skilled artists and craftsmen have produced wares in the true Wedgwood tradition.

Ferguson is now the official spokesperson for Wedgwood, a position that came with a nice fee, originally set at $750,000. She loves the

china, which she has grown up with.

Ferguson started her own collecting trend. With the release of her book and video *Budgie the Little Helicopter*, Budgie collectibles have come into play. Also, many doll collectors want her collectible doll named the Little Red Doll. After the Duchess of York started the Chances for Children mission in 1994, she created Little Red as the logo. Rhonda, a very ill child with an intracranial tumor lying on her optic nerve, inspired the doll; she was also the first child Chances for Children was able to help. The duchess believes that terminally ill children such as that little girl deserve to live their lives as fully as possible. Her charity funded the surgery that helped Rhonda regain her sight. A portion of the proceeds for the colorful and cuddly cloth Little Red doll go to the charity.

Sarah Ferguson *(Courtesy Shooting Stars)*

Top: Sarah Ferguson displays her favorite brand of china.

After spending a little time with Lou Ferrigno, you soon find that the mean monster he portrayed in *The Incredible Hulk* (Bill Bixby's alter ego in the series) is nothing like the actor's true persona. He is really a friendly, soft-hearted person with a genuine love for collecting.

Ferrigno's acting career, in addition to *Hulk,* included two documentaries, an appearance on the series *Trauma Center,* and *Night Court.* When not acting or pumping iron, Ferrigno loves to collect, a hobby of his since childhood (beginning with GI Joes). He has acquired many different items, including antique blowguns and toys. "I collect antique air guns; I shoot the guns. They go way back before firearms were invented. It's amazing: in the old days, they used them like a ball, and they work with air from spring piston. It's becoming very popular and booming in the United States.

"Some of my favorite pieces are made by Holland and Holland Colt and Purdey. I don't really display them, but I do show them to friends that appreciate guns. Some are very old. They have been around since the seventeenth century. It's not easy to find them; they are very hard to get."

His favorite collection comprises a grouping of little cuddly characters filled with beans. You guessed it: Beanie Babies.

"Beanie Babies are what we love. We have an antique turn-of-the-century bookcase and we took all the books out. One of my sons took all of our

The "Incredible Hulk" with his Beanie Baby collection. *(Courtesy Ralph Merlino)*

Beanie Babies and put them in the case. We have over two hundred of them. When you first walk into our house, the first thing you see is the bookcase filled with Beanie Babies." Wife Carla mentioned that they have another antique glass case in her office, which is also filled with Beanie Babies.

"My favorite is the Princess Diana Beanie Baby," Lou Ferrigno stated. "I like all the bears; they have more passion. Princess is my favorite because it reminds me of Princess Diana and how much we all miss her. It brings back good memories of her."

Carla told of a Beanie Baby their friend had acquired. "One of the first ones ever made was the blue elephant. It's going for around five thousand dollars now; however, a friend of mine picked it up for four thousand dollars. I think she's a little crazy, but she thinks she really got a great deal, being able to buy him for four thousand dollars. I guess the blue elephant will just keep going up."

Lou and Carla told me they collect Beanies mainly for their sons. "We collect them for our boys, Lou Jr. and Brent. Brent really loves them."

So, what was the first Beanie Lou ever got? "The first Beanie was the shark, but I'm not sure if we got the Teenie Beanies at McDonald's first and then the larger ones. I think Crunch was the first one we got that was regular size."

Where do they find them? Carla told me, "We buy them ourselves at shows or wherever we can get a good deal. We've never received any as gifts. It doesn't just happen [getting a good collection]. It's a matter of being at the right place at the right time to get good ones. You have to work at this."

Lou's business associate, Joanne Engle, told me about a day she was with Lou at a collector's show. "I was with Lou one time when he bought something for Carla's Barbie collection. It was so cute the way he was checking out all the dolls to find just the right one for her. That was in Gaithersburg, Maryland, and when he finally chose the perfect one, he just said, 'Carla's going to love this one.' It was just so cute

Lou Ferrigno with Incredible Hulk action figures *(Courtesy Ralph Merlino)*

to watch this 6' 5", 290-pound guy checking out the Barbies." That was the same reaction I had watching Lou pick out his Princess Beanie Baby. Many of the collectibles (including Barbies and Beanie Babies) that Lou buys he gets as gifts for his wife and children.

The Incredible Hulk character returned to the big screen in the 2003 film *Hulk*. Universal and Marvel Studios coproduced the flick, which has a computer-generated version of Lou's character. Marvel Media president/CEO Avi Arad said, in a *New York Post* interview, "We'd love to bring Lou in—we love Lou and we think he's wonderful. Lou did a great job for The Hulk and vice versa." Though Lou never collected Hulk memorabilia, Carla has a large collection stored away for a rainy day.

One of the best parts of his work is traveling to different collectors' shows around the country as a special guest. This gives Lou the chance to hunt out new Beanies to add to his collection. Lou told me,

"Every time I travel, I pick up new Beanies for my wife or kids. My kids just love them."

Lou talked about other men he knows who collect Beanies too. "I have friends that are these macho men and they will walk up and tell me about a new Beanie that they picked up for their kids."

Why are Beanies so popular with everyone? Lou explained it this way: "They are unique looking, especially the character versions. Beanies have a mystique to them. In the '70s, the thing that was popular were the GI Joes; in the '80s, it was Miss Piggy; and in the late '90s and early [twenty-first century], it's Beanie Babies."

I asked Lou and Carla to sum up what Beanie Babies meant to them. For Carla, the answer was, "I've met so many wonderful people doing this. I remember having a bad day, so I'd go looking for Beanie Babies, and during that quest, I would meet some of the nicest people. We'd have fun, share, and make friends. It's more than just collecting; it's an adventure."

Lou said he enjoys seeing other people's collections, even though it makes him a little jealous when he sees ones that he doesn't have. "Seeing other's collections brings me joy, but it's still like a contest," stated Lou. "You're always trying to outdo the other people and get ones that you don't have. The best part about collecting Beanie Babies is that its something we can do as a family. I love buying Beanies for my kids and they love them. It's something we can sit around as a family and talk about. We will all discuss the different characters and which ones we like the best; it's nice. Collecting Beanie Babies brings us together as a family. There's a bonding there."

When you think of a policeman, a detective, or the cop on the beat, you probably draw the image of actor Dennis Franz. Franz has played more than nineteen police officers in his long career. Besides acting, Franz's second love is collecting. This self-proclaimed pack rat is the ultimate collector in every sense of the word.

His Emmy Award- and Golden Globe Award-winning portrayal of Andy Sipowicz on the hit television series *NYPD Blue* was of a tough cop, yet his true persona is one of a friendly, down-to-earth guy who can make anyone feel instantly comfortable. A self-confessed Martha Stewart devotee, he spends his weekends scouring garage sales and flea markets with his wife and fellow collector, Joanie Zeck.

Of his collecting obsession, Franz states that he has been a collector all his life. "Even when I was kid, I collected things like baseball cards and marbles and other types of cards, so it really began way back then. I've turned into a pack rat as the years have gone on. When I was in the service, I was the pack rat who would always carry the extra amount of all the C rations. I'd pick things up in Vietnam and collect whatever souvenirs I could find and lug another fifty pounds of stuff on my back. Collecting has always been something that's been with me."

Franz is not alone in his collecting ventures. His wife, Joanie, is also a collector. According to Franz, "She has always been collecting stuff, for as long as I can remember. At one time, it was little animals.

Dennis Franz with his wife, Joanie *(AP Photo)*

Once she went through her 'cow period.' She collected anything with cows: paintings, pictures—anything in the shape of a cow—big wooden carvings, miniatures, ceramics, and bottles with cows on [them]. It got ridiculous after a while, so she switched to pigs. We were inundated with all this pig stuff! Then we switched to collecting colored bowls, and big marble balls that sat on pedestals. Then we switched again on my fiftieth birthday, and we started collecting containers and boxes."

Once word got out that Franz was now collecting boxes, he started receiving them as gifts. "I received some fascinating boxes. Some are like jigsaw boxes. . . . You open up this master case and inside there are other little compartments. People used boxes for a variety of reasons, such as old jewelry and tins. I like them all."

Dennis and Joanie aren't specific on the kinds of things they collect. But Americana does top their list. According to Franz, "If it has a story behind it that we find fascinating, and it's something that's been used in the past, then we'd be attracted to it. We have a coffee table in our den that was once a chicken incubator for baby chicks. It makes for a nice conservation piece! It had a little stove in it. I'm not sure what that was used for. Old washing machines, butter churns—that's the kind of stuff we like."

When Dennis and Joanie told friends that they were interested in Depression glass, their collection grew by leaps and bounds. "Joanie wanted to collect pink or green glass. Within no time, we had such a major collection of Depression glass that we knew we'd have to be more specific. Over the last couple of years, we've been looking for Jadite. It's a little harder to find. We try to match patterns."

To add to all of his other collections, Franz started collecting Chicago Cubs memorabilia. "I will always be a Cub fan. I was an avid Cub fan as a boy and grew up wanting to be Ernie Banks. I actually got the pleasure of getting to meet and know Ernie. I also have some old baseball cards that I collected when I was young. They weren't as easy to get then as they are now. You'd get a pack for a nickel with a big slab of gum and a couple of cards in them. I'd trade and swap them until I got whole sets. It wasn't easy to do. I managed to collect several years of cards."

His friends didn't let him down in the sports category either. Fellow acting buddy Michael Harney, who played Mike Roberts from *NYPD Blue*, gave Dennis a very unique baseball card of Ernie Banks. "It's six inches by six inches square and has a nice picture of Ernie on the front, with his statistics on the back. It was a 45-rpm record. It even still had the hole in the center, where the record went, which meant it had never been played. So, even

ERNIE BANKS

This signed Ernie Banks baseball card was a gift to the actor from the author. Franz loves to collect Ernie Banks items.

though it was old, it was brand new. It's a valuable little piece," stated Franz. He also has an autographed ball from Ernie.

Franz also loves to shop auctions for his goodies. So is it hard searching for bargains when you're a celebrity? "Yes, people recognize me, but it doesn't stop me from bargaining!"

While Franz will admit he gets detoured easily at the sight of a garage-sale sign, and says, "My house is decorated in early swap meet," he does try to stick with his favorites, which include Americana and Jadite dishes. He has been known to pick up a few extra sets of golf clubs as well. According to Franz, "I use a lot of them, thinking it will help my game!"

JUICY TIDBIT

It looks like writing is something Tom Hanks enjoys. It appears he not only acts, but also likes to hit a few keys, and I'm not talking about piano keys. Hanks collects typewriters, and from what I've been told, he prefers the old manual style to the fancy, new electrics. Hanks told *Country Living*, "I like old manual typewriters that were made prior to the Second World War. I keep them by the telephone and I use them to write notes to my friends. They usually cost me about $45 apiece—and another $125 to get them back into working order!"

Sarah Michelle Gellar is best known for her starring role in the television series *Buffy the Vampire Slayer.* Gellar is a lover of antique books. No, they don't have to have anything to do with vampires! I've been told that one of her favorite places to shop is Heritage Bookstore, and she rarely steps out empty handed.

For many people, books are a great escape, and that is true with Gellar. She was quoted by Homestore.com as saying, "I cannot go into the Heritage Bookstore without buying something. I joke, it's my church. Whenever I'm having a bad day, I can go in there and look at these books and get completely lost in the old illustrative art. One of my favorite books that I own is a first edition of *Les Liaisons Dangereux* [Gellar starred in the film *Cruel Intentions,* a contemporary adaptation of this book], which was a very, very difficult thing to find. I had to locate it on the Internet. I have the book in French and English."

Gellar also loves children's books. Any children's illustrated book may catch her eye, but a few of her favorites are a collection by J. M. Barrie, including *Peter and Wendy* and *Peter Pan in Kensington Gardens.* One famous early illustrator, Arthur Rackham, illustrated this series, while many other illustrators have put their work to the same book at various dates. "It's a complete collection of his works. It's a boxed set. They're bound in white and they are exquisite," Gellar told Homestore.com. It's a collection that perhaps Gellar may share with her children someday.

Sarah Michelle Gellar *(AP Photo)*

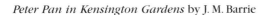

Peter Pan in Kensington Gardens by J. M. Barrie

It's no secret that popular actress and comedienne Whoopi Goldberg is a big collector of Bakelite jewelry. Bakelite is a revolutionary, nonflammable early plastic that made a splash in the 1920s, 1930s, and 1940s. Whoopi's favorite pieces are Bakelite bracelets, which she wears frequently. She also likes prints by Maxfield Parrish, the popular artist from the early 1920s and 1930s who uses beautiful shades of blue in his work. I've been told that Goldberg also collects art and rare books, particularly rare editions framed in gold and children's books. So, she is definitely a diversified collector. Goldberg also owns a General Electric Bandy doll just like mine. This rare composition doll was sold in the 1930s and retails today for between one thousand and fifteen hundred dollars.

Whoopi Goldberg *(Courtesy Shooting Stars)*

Whoopi owns a Bandy doll just like the author's.

DID YOU KNOW?

Celebrities and jewelry go hand in hand. Joan Crawford, the Duchess of Windsor, Ava Gardner, Mary Pickford, and several other celebrities can be seen in many color and black-and-white photos wearing jewels.

Pickford was never shown on film wearing more jewelry than a string of pearls. This was done to preserve her image of innocence, but in real life, she preferred very large rubies and star sapphires. In fact, Pickford once owned both the sixty-carat "Star of Bombay" and the two-hundred-carat "Star of India." And she was not shy about wearing them both at the same time.

Joan Crawford loved sapphires and large stones, including a bracelet set with three star sapphires of 73.15 carats, 63.61 carats, and 57.65 carats. Her second husband gave her a seventy-carat star sapphire engagement ring, and she owned a seventy-two-carat, emerald-cut sapphire.

Marlene Dietrich wore jewels in several of her films (remember her role as the jewel thief in *Desire* in 1938?). The ruby bracelet she wore in the film *Stage Fright* sold at Sotheby's for $990,000. Many celebrities, including those named above, have their own favorite jewelry designers.

Marlene Dietrich

What better way to relax than to come home to the blue water and swimming fish of your own fish tank? Actor Steve Guttenberg, an avid collector of saltwater fish, does just that. "I've been collecting for about fifteen years now," Guttenberg told me. "I started collecting when I would be out surfing." Guttenberg would see beautiful saltwater fish, and he decided he wanted to have them at home as well.

While many fish are beautiful, today's collectors, including Guttenberg, are looking for more than just beauty. The sight of swimming fish is said to be a stress reliever and creates good karma. Other fish fans include Paula Abdul, Tommy Lee Jones, Jerry Seinfeld, Greg Louganis, Burt Reynolds, Robert Wagner, and Aaron Spelling. The hobby can be expensive. While some fish, like an American comet goldfish, cost about ten cents (they live up to six months), a grand champion Japanese koi (which has about a seventy-year life span) can run as high as one hundred thousand dollars. Some fish enthusiasts, like James Cameron and Tim Allen, have actually owned their own live reefs. The price tags on those start around fifteen thousand dollars.

Steve Guttenberg (*Courtesy Shooting Stars*)

Steve relieves stress by watching his collection of saltwater fish. (*Courtesy Ripley's Aquarium of the Smokies*)

ROBERT DAVID HALL
GUITARS

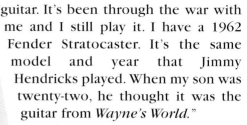

Robert David Hall, who stars as Coroner Dr. Robbins on the CBS hit *CSI: Crime Scene Investigation* is not only a gifted actor but also a collector. His collection of choice is guitars.

A character actor, Hall has had an extensive twenty-year career during which he has amassed numerous credits in film and television. His feature film work has included roles in F. Gary Gray's *The Negotiator,* starring Kevin Spacey and Samuel L. Jackson; Paul Verhoeven's *Starship Troopers,* starring Casper van Dien and Denise Richards; and Michael Apted's *Class Action,* starring Gene Hackman and Laurence Fishburne. Hall has also appeared on the television series *The West Wing* and has played recurring roles on *Family Law* and *The Practice.*

Robert David Hall with one of the guitars in his collection. *(Courtesy Robert David Hall and Cynthia Snyder Public Relations)*

One of the most prominent disabled actors working today, in 1978 Hall was struck by an tractor-trailer while in his car and was severely injured. After several months in a burn unit and the amputation of both legs, he today walks comfortably on two prosthetic limbs.

In addition to acting, Hall's passions include music and voice work as well as playing the guitar. A former band member, Hall was also once the music director of KNX-FM, a legendary CBS alternative music station in Los Angeles.

"I've been playing stringed musical instruments since I was eight," Hall told me. "My wife accuses me of loving my guitars more than her but, it's a different kind of love. My wife, Judy, is a cellist, and I always wanted to play the guitar. I am old enough to be sucked in by Elvis and Gene Autry."

Hall went from playing by himself to joining bands. "Over the years I played in bands and all kinds of music. I've collected different instruments over the years. I bought my first excellent guitar when I was eighteen, a 000-28 Martin made in 1955. I bought it in 1965. I still own that

guitar. It's been through the war with me and I still play it. I have a 1962 Fender Stratocaster. It's the same model and year that Jimmy Hendricks played. When my son was twenty-two, he thought it was the guitar from *Wayne's World.*"

Other items in Robert's collection include a 1963 0-16 New Yorker Model Martin (parlor guitar), a late '50s/early '60s D-28 Martin, a 1957 Fender Telecaster Fender Base guitar, two Hawaiian ukuleles that are about twenty-five years old and two mandolins built by one of his oldest and closest friends, Michael Dulak. "He has a mandolin company in Missouri. He's well known," stated Robert.

So with such a wide assortment of instruments, which is his favorite?

"My favorite electric is my '62 white Stratocaster and my favorite acoustic is a 000-28 Martin," stated Robert.

Robert starting collecting at a fairly young age, "I hounded my parents for a guitar when I saw Elvis playing it. My brother played drums and we drove my dad crazy." Now, his collection is displayed in a special music room in his home. "We can leave the guitars out in there so I can just walk in and play them," said Robert. "I leave a couple out at a time but I'm not a collector who leaves them locked in a room, I baby them."

Getting a good deal on a guitar isn't always easy to do. "My wife, Judy, can walk in and find the few things that are worth something. If I see an instrument I usually know if it is a good one. It seems even eighty-five-year-old grandmothers know the value of their good guitars these days. It's hard to find a bargain." Robert buys his guitars the old fashioned way, through retail stores. "Usually I get them from guitar stores that I worked at when I was young. I'd take acting lessons. Play at night in bands. I spent most of my twenties as a musician. I loved playing music.

His advice for other collectors is simple, "Love what you do. Learn everything you can about instruments. There are a million great books out there and there is no excuse not to know what you're looking for. An instrument that looks great may not play well. If it's rare and plays well—jump on it if you can."

I had the pleasure to meet with actor George Hamilton while he was in the Orlando area one winter. He was at Disney World and was planning to read at the candlelight procession that evening. Casually dressed in a white tee shirt and jeans, he was as attractive in person as he appears in film. Hamilton personifies the golden age of Hollywood with his style, charm, and good looks. George Hamilton's films have included *All the Fine Young Cannibals* (1960, with Natalie Wood), *Evel* (1971, as daredevil Evel Knievel), and Francis Ford Coppola's *The Godfather, Part III* (1990). In the 1990s, Hamilton opened a chain of upscale cigar bars and coffee clubs.

When I asked him what he collected, he started to smile. "All kinds of things, cuff links, hatpins, stickpins, and cigar labels. I'll collect something for awhile, and then I'll get rid of it and move on to something else." Thinking back to when he was a young boy, he told with a grin a story about a doll collection and his childhood home. "My brother walked into this room that was filled with old dolls. They sat there lined up looking out at him, and it scared him to death. He never wanted to go back into that room with the dolls."

Hamilton said that one of his favorite collections is his accumulation of cigar labels. "I have all different kinds and they make a nice collection as well as a good conversation piece." He said he wasn't sure how he started collecting hatpins and stickpins, but that the cuff links were a collection he could actually use if he wanted. "They certainly come in handy at times."

George Hamilton

Cigar labels are just one of the types of items that George collects.

The lights come on, the music begins, and out on the ice whips a man dressed in a sparkling costume, with a smile so contagious you can't help but smile with him. Scott Hamilton is clearly one of the most beloved and most popular figure-skating stars in the world today. He is perpetually bridging the gap between sports and entertainment. Hamilton's "anything is possible" attitude is prevalent in his role as entertainer, role model, and cancer survivor. Despite such demands, Hamilton has managed to find time for one more thing, collecting pinball machines.

When asked how he started collecting pinball machines, Hamilton answered, "Well, I've always liked games. Video and pinball games. I'd be on the road, and it would be a good way to pass time. I find with a lot of videos it's easy to memorize them, and there wasn't a random quality to them. So, I started playing pinball, and I liked it so much that I decided that I had space in my house for a machine, and I thought I'd start collecting them." To date, Hamilton has six machines in his collection. He started collecting several years ago and has tried to get a new one almost every year.

Hamilton says he plays all the time at both his homes—in Denver and in L.A. When asked if he was any good, he told me, "It's funny, because I've put all six high scores on every one of the games.

There is a lady that comes over that helps clean the house, and there is a game that she likes to play. She keeps threatening to put the high score on it. Every time she puts a score on, I play to make sure she doesn't have a score on there anymore. She's probably going to figure out how to reset the high scores, but until she does, I'll have the high scores!" Hamilton shares the games with his friends and says it's fun to see who can get the top scores.

While pinball machines are an interesting collection, they can be pricey. "They are expensive. That's the hard part about collecting them. It's hard for people to afford them," said Hamilton, stating that the average game runs around four thousand dollars. "It makes it hard to justify buying them, so I stick with one a year."

Hamilton said he'd like to add an *X-Files* game to his collection. "I had the pleasure of meeting David Duchovny a few times, and he's really a nice guy."

So, what else would Scott Hamilton like to collect if given the chance? He says, "If I had all the money in the world, I'd collect Porsches and pinball machines. But I don't have all the money in the world, so I'm going to have to stick with pinball machines!"

Above: Scott Hamilton *(Courtesy Scott Hamilton and Michael Sterling & Assoc.)*

Pinball machines are unusual but fun items to collect.

The Hard Rock Café has one of the biggest collections of rock-'n'-roll and movie memorabilia in the world. It is a pop-culture paradise with everything from Jayne Mansfield's bathing suit to a selection of autographed guitars from some of the country's biggest stars. It has over 108 restaurants in forty-eight countries, with memorabilia in each location. The chain also has a huge warehouse of memorabilia, with over forty thousand items worth millions of dollars.

The original site of the first Hard Rock in London was a Rolls-Royce dealership. Princess Diana was a Hard Rock fan, and she had been spotted several times wearing a Hard Rock leather jacket. Paul McCartney played his first post-Beatles gig at the London Hard Rock in 1973.

Various celebrities donate many of the collectibles found in the cafés. Aerosmith donated a huge collection of memorabilia to the Boston Hard Rock in conjunction with their multi-platinum release of *Pump* and dubbed it the Aerosmithsonian Collection. Peter Townshend of The Who smashed his last guitar outside the London Hard Rock on October 3, 1989, and the remains are now displayed inside the restaurant.

Singer and songwriter Sir Elton John is a collector of many things. He told *Interview*, "I have always been an accumulator—but I haven't always been a collector in the fullest sense." John said he collected Art Nouveau from the 1970s as well as photographs. He also has a passion for scented candles. According to *InStyle*, John's London home has a special closet for a collection of over two hundred candles, which he oversees. He told *InStyle*, "I can't imagine a room without candles." Some of his favorite scents include vanilla, lily of the valley, tuberose, and sandlewood, and he changes them with the seasons. The candle maker Slatkin & Company produced a special Elton candle, with a percentage of its sales being donated to the Elton John AIDS Foundation, which funds patient-care services for people living with HIV and AIDS. John even teamed up with the crystal company Lalique to produce the Elton's Angel. The crystal piece, which retailed for $375, was the first in a series. The small crystal cherub is hand painted with twenty-four-karat gold enameling. Lalique donated 5 percent of the sales to his charity.

It has been reported that though he rarely drives, John has a collection of luxury automobiles, including four Bentleys and a Jaguar XJ220 worth more than six hundred thousand dollars. Other items he collects include art, eyeglasses, furniture, lamps, and jukeboxes, and according to sources, he buys items by the truckload.

To many, John is known as the "King of Costumes." His eyeglasses per tour have been estimated to cost more than forty thousand dollars. His shoes and costumes would put even Liberace to shame. When the entertainer was "cleaning his closet" in 1988, Sotheby's auction house gave him a hand. Fans could bid on his fabulous specs, platform shoes, or outrageous costumes. Among the highlights of the auction was a pink Eiffel Tower hat. The hat is valued in the thousands of dollars. Other items included the boots worn by John in the film *Tommy* and shoes with heels as high as eight inches. The Hard Rock Café purchased many of the shoes, and they can be seen throughout their many restaurants.

Elton John discusses an upcoming exhibit of his photography collection during a news conference at a New York hotel. *(AP Photo)*

Actress Angelina Jolie has always been a little bit different. Beautiful, with a mind of her own, this Best Actress Award winner has a collection of knives and daggers. Jolie began collecting knives as a young girl after attending a Renaissance fair. "I have a collection, yes," stated Jolie. "I keep them in a case." Jolie told Barbara Walters during an *ABC 20/20* interview, "I've always been fascinated by other cultures and history and honor and fight and so they . . . they are not shiny, brand-new sharp knives from the store. They're antique beautiful knives from other countries, and they are locked in a case so my son does not touch them." Jolie has collected a scar or two from knives as well, including an *X* on her arm. Besides knives, Jolie has a collection of body tattoos. Hopefully, she'll keep the tattoos to a minimum and just stick with knives. She's much too pretty to be marked up.

Angelina Jolie *(AP Photo)*

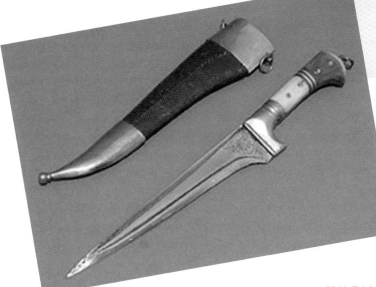

Angelina has a collection of antique knives similar to this one.

JUICY TIDBIT!

What do Sally Jesse Raphael and Tom Snyder have in common? They both like toy trains.

Beautiful and talented Naomi Judd has a collection of tiaras that started with her daughters Wynonna and Ashley calling her "the queen of everything." The Grammy Award-winning singer of the group The Judds, which includes her motorcycle-riding daughter Wynonna, received her first tiara from an estate sale in Tennessee. Others soon followed, with her daughters buying them for her as gifts. Naomi told me, "In the mid-'80s, a girlfriend gave me a tiara that a debutante had won in Memphis, Tennessee. She purchased it at an estate sale because Wynonna and Ashley had taken to calling me, 'the queen of everything.' Patty placed it on my head and said, 'After all a queen must have a royal crown.' Having raised Wynonna and Ashley alone, my daughters thought I knew everything.

"Wye and I were touring year round as The Judds, performing in a different city every night. We had requested that the Make-A-Wish Foundation send children to our concert and then come backstage afterwards. And so it was, a ceremony was born. To encourage these children, whose days were spent in hospitals undergoing treatments, Wye and I started to play upon our celebrity. With a child seated on our bus, the *Dream Chaser,* Wynonna would announce me as 'Her Royal Highness—The Queen of Everything.' With appropriate trumpet noise, I would dramatically burst upon the scene in my splendid over-the-top stage costume. The rhyme we wrote went something like 'Mecca lecca high, Mecca lecca highnee ho, you are safe and loved wherever you may go.' If the parents granted permission, we would sing 'Jesus Loves Me' with the child or some appropriate familiar tune. Our desire was to razzle-dazzle them with something to take them out of their dreary trial.

"I was driving by this small trophy shop in our town of Franklin, Tennessee, when I realized I could get a bigger crown and a rhinestone scepter. The magic wand helped me follow through on [Wynonna's] announcement for 'fear be gone' to banish their doubts and dreads. In our travel I came upon

Naomi Judd *(Courtesy Naomijudd.com)*

Naomi feels like the queen of everything when she wears tiaras.

a variety of sizes and styles of tiaras down through the years. One of my favorites is an art deco vintage piece Wynonna found for me in Los Angeles. Ashley gave me an understated elegant tiara that I wore to an award show ceremony.

"One late afternoon I heard my deluxe diva daughter Wynonna roar up to the backyard of my farm on her Fatboy Harley Davidson motorcycle. I was barefoot doing housework in my 100 percent cotton at-home clothes. I had on no makeup and hadn't brushed my hair, which was pulled back in a ponytail. I [dashed] to the closet and got my most outlandish crown. Wynonna was at home with me for hours, helped me cook dinner, did the supper dishes, and drove away into the night without ever even acknowledging that I was wearing this huge honkin' rhinestone crown.

"It has been one of the greatest privileges of my life that down through the last twenty years of entertaining, the public has come to view me as a bit of a fairy godmother because I try to instill hope and sell people on themselves. Every chance I get I remind people that they are smarter than they think; they are and stronger than they give themselves credit for. I have a little Glinda the Good Witch figurine that sits on my windowsill. It was a gift from Wynonna during our farewell tour. People with all manner of illnesses and problems came to visit with me and seek works of wisdom and guidance. Wynonna called it, 'wishing upon a star.' What I leave with that individual is a sense that self-esteem is their answer. As Glinda told Dorothy in the *Wizard of Oz,* 'You have the power all alone.'"

Tiaras aren't the only thing that Naomi has a love for. Her collecting interests also include reproduction paintings by Maxfield Parrish, an early American illustrator known for his vivid blues and greens. Looking down the stairwell of her home, one can see a wide assortment of his work, as it fills the walls.

This actor has a real ball with collecting. Richard Karn is known to most of us as Al Borland, Tim Allen's sidekick on the hit television sitcom *Home Improvement*. The series, which lasted eight seasons, was the crowning jewel of Richard's work as an actor. Besides acting, Richard has another love: golf. His love for the game (he has a twenty handicap) leads him on the journey of collecting items related to the sport.

While hanging out on the nation's courses, Karn has picked up a thing or two, not tips, but golf balls, of which he has a sizable collection. Karn's collection is modest in price but modern and personal. It consists of balls signed by celebrities Karn has met at golf tournaments, both the charity events he hosts and those he attended as a celebrity himself. I spoke with Karn as he returned from the Crosby Golf Tournament in Winston-Salem, North Carolina, and we discussed his collection in detail.

Karn has been collecting since the late 1980s. "I have several favorite pieces. One signed by Bob Hope and another by Gerald Ford, who I played with. I have another ball signed by Arnold Palmer," stated Karn. When asked how he shows his collection off, Karn stated, "I have a golf-ball rack that my wife bought me for Christmas. It only has room for about 80 balls. That holds most of my collection, which is currently around 120. I have a lot of my own celebrity golf balls from the Richard Karn Celebrity Golf Classic, balls by Titleist that I have celebrities sign." When asked if he collects antique golf memorabilia (I heard Arnold Schwarzenegger is a big fan of this category of collectible), he told me,

"That's not part of my collection, antique golf balls. Maybe the older balls will be next for me."

Karn says the meanings behind the balls are important. "I've played at some nice courses, so I'll get a logo ball. Or if I run into somebody like Phil Mickelson, I'll have him sign a ball for me." He said his favorite brand of ball is Titleist. "They were one of the sponsors for my golf tournament. They gave me balls with my name printed on them. I have to be really careful with them because if you lose a ball, and your name is on it, people are going to say, 'Wow, look how bad he was! I can't believe this ball ended up here.'"

What's the most interesting thing that happened to him while trying to add to his collection? "I was at the AT&T Golf Tournament up in Pebble Beach when I saw Phil Mickelson. I walked up to him and said, 'Phil, would you sign my golf ball?' And he looked at me and said, 'I'm sorry, I don't sign golf balls.' And I said, 'Oh, okay.' His wife is standing next to him and she's hitting him and saying, 'It's okay, you can do this.' Phil is looking at his wife like, 'What are you talking about? I'm not signing the golf ball.' So I said, 'Fine,' and I walked away. About five seconds later, he runs up to me and says, 'I'm sorry, my wife told me who you are and I didn't realize. You know a lot of people just take these balls and go sell them somewhere.' Then he took my ball and signed it for me." Karn said signing a golf ball isn't easy. "It takes a knack. I've signed a few in my day."

So, what's left for Karn to acquire? "I'd like to get quite a few more signed balls from the tour players, Tiger Woods and others. I wouldn't just go and a buy a ball with someone's name on it at a store. My collection is more along the lines of people I've come in contact with. That's what makes it special."

Above: Richard Karn *(Courtesy Richard Karn and StarDays)*

Below: Autographed golf balls, like the one signed by Arnold Palmer, are Richard Karn's favorite collectibles.

Champagne wishes and caviar dreams is what this collector is known for. His caviar dreams include finding another paperweight to add to his collection, and his favorites are the pieces that contain marine life. He buys most of his paperweights through L. H. Selman, Ltd., a dealer in Santa Cruz, California, that specializes in selling beautiful glass artworks.

"Paperweights come in all shapes and designs," explains Leach. "I have narrowed my collection to paperweights with seascapes, tropical fish, and marine life." Leach's retirement home, located on a private island called Jumby Bay on the beautiful waters off the coast of Antigua, West Indies, is his sanctuary. The home sits on three acres with ocean frontage. States Leach, "I miss it when I'm not there. I love being surrounded by the sea." When not at home, Leach's New York office is where he spends a great deal of his time. It's also where many pieces of his collection are housed; others are kept in an illuminated cabinet in his home in Connecticut.

In 1983, Leach launched *Lifestyles of the Rich and Famous,* which he followed in 1986 with *Fame, Fortune and Romance* for ABC-TV, *Runaway with the Rich and Famous* in 1987, and *Home Video of the Stars* in 1993. *Lifestyles,* after thirteen unprecedented seasons, is seen in over thirty countries around the world.

Many paperweights can be purchased for under a hundred dollars, while others can sell for more than nine thousand dollars. Leach has over one hundred paperweights in his collection. To him, they

Robin Leach posing in front of a background of his marine paperweights. *(Courtesy Leach Entertainment)*

are a work of art. He continues to look for unique pieces to add to his collection. Leach states, "Hosting *Lifestyles of the Rich and Famous* has allowed me to visit many exotic places and, at the same time, add to my collection." Is there anything special he is still looking for? Robin states that it's quality, not quantity, that persuades him to buy. If it's beautiful and contains marine life, then it's worth adding to his collection.

"I started collecting when I saw a photograph in a mail-order catalog. From that initial purchase I now have over 150 but I only collect those with undersea life." Leach has been collecting for many years now. "I'll buy them in all shapes and sizes; ovals, circular, etc. While I keep most in Antigua I also have them at my house in Connecticut to remind me I should be down on a sunny beach instead of working too hard."

Creating glass paperweights is truly an art. "I think that working with glass and what glass artists do with paperweights is the most difficult, and most challenging, of the creative process. It can take up to twelve weeks to make one paperweight. I have a respect and admiration for the artist for what is a difficult art form and, to me, one of the most beautiful." Leach continued, "Any artist who can sit down and successfully make a detailed seascape paperweight is regarded as a genius to me."

"You can find them at county fairs, antique auctions, and sales occasionally, but I buy a majority of my paperweights from Larry Selman at L. H. Selman, Ltd., and I have looked through art galleries on Madison Avenue. I don't buy from flea markets, general sales, or the Internet. I can't remember the first one I bought, but one in my collection is in the shape of a black hollowed-out egg that lights up from underneath to show the artist's interpretation of the ocean and its life at nighttime. I have also started a small miniature collection (only about 2" high, 3" wide) of etched paper-weights showing skylines of various cities around the world and their key architectural attraction, like the Empire State Building, Tour Eiffel, etc. I add one each year at Christmas and birthdays to keep the collection growing. These are displayed on the staircase walls above my glass antique cabinet with my paperweight collection at my Las Vegas home. I also have two antique paperweights from the old school of swirls, but they are not in my seascape collection cabinet. They are family heirlooms that sit on the bookcase."

Leach, I'm sure, will be looking for another paperweight to add to his collection while traveling up to three hundred days and over two hundred fifty thousand miles a year. He will have plenty of ground to cover looking for the beauties. He closed by saying, "I will keep adding to my seascape collection anytime I find something unique and different from what I already have."

MORE ABOUT PAPERWEIGHTS

According to L. H. Selman, Ltd., a leader in the paper-weight-collecting field, kings and queens collected glass paperweights. Later, Oscar Wilde and Truman Capote acquired and wrote of them. Truman Capote carried his favorites with him in a small black bag. Others who collected paperweights were Queen Victoria, King Faruk of Egypt, and Queen Mary. Today, many celebrities and well-known personalities collect or own paper-weights, including former president Bill Clinton, actor Andy Griffith, director John Landis, astronaut Alan Shepard, and NBC correspondent Irving R. Levine.

Bill Clinton (Courtesy Kyle Cassidy)

An example of the beautiful marine paper-weights that Robin Leach keeps in his home. *(Courtesy L. H. Selman, Ltd.)*

Singer Brenda Lee is an original. A child prodigy, Lee has been performing since she was seven years old and was one of the biggest pop stars of the early '60s, selling more than one hundred million albums. She's even sung at the Grand Ole Opry with Elvis Presley. She continues to work nearly every day of the year, singing with her unique voice and style.

Lee told me she is a big collector. She collects a wide array of items, including Armani figures, old Capodimonte porcelain figures, and crystal by such companies as Waterford, Baccarat, and Lalique. "I collect everything," explained Lee, "antique fans, Imari porcelain, every kind of doll you could think of, snow babies, old perfume bottles, silver frames, jade, wood block prints, and I'm just getting started." Lee said that some of her favorite pieces are boxes. "I collect all sorts of boxes made out of various materials, including porcelain and wood. I've always loved pretty things and then one day I got into miniatures. My collecting just went from there. I started collecting Victorian dollhouses, and I would put the miniature pieces that I bought in them. I have a pretty extensive collection." Our mutual friend Eddie Morelli told me, "Every space in Brenda's house is filled with collectibles. She has some wonderful things."

Lee said she has been collecting since the '80s. "It's hard for me to pick any favorites. I love them all. Many of the pieces I own, people have given to me and that gives them a sentimental value."

Brenda Lee with her Victorian dollhouses. *(Courtesy Brenda Lee)*

Brenda Lee's porcelain collectibles. *(Courtesy Brenda Lee)*

Talk-show host Jay Leno is known not only for being a great comedian but also for his love of cars. Leno followed in the footsteps of legendary NBC late-night hosts Steve Allen, Jack Paar, and Johnny Carson and is currently the host of the Emmy Award-winning and top-rated *The Tonight Show with Jay Leno.*

His vehicle collection (mainly classic cars) consists of more than one hundred (and counting) vehicles, including cars and motorcycles, which he houses in a seventeen-thousand-square-foot converted airplane hangar. He is one of the world's premier car and motorcycle collectors and restorers, as well as an authority on the subject. Leno has even written for *Popular Mechanics* several times.

The toy company Mattel produced a series of cars known as the Hot Wheels Legends Jay Leno Collection. The first issue had four die-cast cars, which were all selected for their cutting-edge technology and eye-catching design. These miniature versions of Leno's great loves could be purchased at local toy stores and featured some of Leno's favorites, including a Lamborghini Miura, a Jaguar XKE, a Shelby Cobra replica, and a Shelby Mustang GT 350.

One of Leno's favorite life-size pieces includes a 1941 American LaFrance fire truck, which he has stated can cruise seventy-five to eighty miles per hour on the freeway. Other notables in Leno's collection are Bugattis, Duisenbergs, and a 1913 Mercer Raceabout. Paparazzi have a field day—with Leno standing outside his home or near the entrance to his studio—trying to see which automobile or motorcycle Leno will be driving on any certain day.

Few car collectors are as passionate about their hobby as Leno. He's very open and will take time to answer questions about his various vehicles. His collection has nearly doubled in the last few years, a clear sign that this collection isn't even close to slowing down. Leno said he's always loved cars, even as a kid. Leno told the *Robb Report,* "Most guys in this business have thirty-five women and one car. I've got one woman and thirty-five cars, and it's a lot cheaper." He also stated, "I can remember [my father] telling stories about going somewhere and saying, 'Oh, this Packard went by, and it was as long as a city block, and it was shiny black,' and in my mind I thought, well, that's the car to have. Why would you want a mid-'60s car when you can get yourself a Packard, because that's what would impress my father. So maybe the cars I like are more a reflection of my dad."

On various days, Leno will drive a different car to the NBC studios in Burbank, California. His cars range from brand-new versions to classic antiques. Leno decides which car to purchase based on what appeals to him and which ones he is able to work on. According to Napsnet.com, Leno started working on cars at age fourteen. The first was a thirty-year-old pickup truck that he restored and kept in repair to drive up and down his parent's driveway for two years while practicing for his driver's test. In an interview with Napsnet.com, Leno joked, "Fortunately, it was a long driveway."

Leno told the *Robb Report,* "Car collecting is something I enjoy doing, and I expect to lose money on it. My philosophy is, if you're making money in the sport, you're doing it wrong! I hope I don't lose a lot, but if I get to the point where I have to sell them . . . well, by that time, when I have to sell my cars, by that time the house and everything else is already gone, so I'm in a lot of trouble!"

With Leno's popularity, I don't see him being forced to sell his car collection anytime soon. It would be nice if Leno could put his amazing collection in a museum so others could enjoy seeing it. And yes, Jay, you could always sneak them out and give them a spin around the block.

Top: The Tonight Show host, Jay Leno, poses with a copy of his children's book, *If Roast Beef Could Fly,* in Burbank, California, surrounded by his automobiles. *(AP Photo)*

Bottom: Jay Leno loves autos, but he also has several motorcycles in his collection. *(AP Photo)*

Do you remember being a little kid and thinking how great something was? Then, after you grew up, did you begin collecting that very item? Or, perhaps, your collecting obsession started as a child and never went away. That's the case with collector and movie historian Leonard Maltin. "When I was little, maybe eight or nine, my parents took me to see the movie *The Golden Age of Comedy.* It had clips of Chaplin, Laurel and Hardy, and all the great comedians. That is when my love of movies and movie memorabilia all started."

Maltin has been a film historian and correspondent for *Entertainment Tonight* since the early '80s. The show, which Maltin joined on May 28, 1982, is the number one entertainment newsmagazine in syndication. Besides working on *Entertainment Tonight,* and cohosting a weekly movie review show, *Hot Ticket,* Maltin keeps himself busy with several projects. He teaches at the University of Southern California, in the Cinema-TV Department. He has penned a number of cinema-related books, including *Leonard Maltin's Family Film Guide, Leonard Maltin's Movie & Video Guide* (considered a standard film reference around the world), *The Great American Broadcast, Of Mice & Magic: A History of American Animated Cartoons, The Great Movie Comedians,* and *The Disney Films,* to name a few.

Growing up in New Jersey, Maltin would often find himself frequenting an old bookstore in Hackensack, New Jersey. "It was a fun place to go and

Leonard Maltin *(Courtesy Leonard Maltin)*

look around. That's where I found a portrait of D. W. Griffith done in a sepia tint on a heavy stock. I had to have it. To this day, I haven't seen another one like it," recalls Maltin. "One day a local library was having a sale of its old books, and I found one by Theodore Huff on Charlie Chaplin, from 1951. I paid ten cents for it. That was my first book related to the movies." Around the same time, his parents purchased a picture book called *The Movies* for him, and his collection was on its way. He would add to it by visiting New York City and an area on Fourth Avenue fondly known as "Book Row." While there, Maltin would shop at the Strand Bookstore, located on Broadway. "There were thousands of books there. And I really enjoyed going. That store is still there today," states Maltin.

Recalling how his collection expanded from books to movie stills, Maltin explains, "The first picture I bought was Charlie Chaplin, and I just kept on buying. Now, I have thousands of stills." Expressing his love of movies and movie stills, Maltin states, "I started collecting the movie stills when I was twelve or thirteen. At the time, I could buy them for twenty-five cents or thirty-five cents. The most I paid was fifty cents. It was a fun and affordable hobby. The reproduction technique was not as good then as it is today." Maltin began having his stills autographed at the tender age of thirteen, long before autographed pictures were the craze. "One time that comes to mind, I had the day off from school, and I went into Manhattan. Buster Keaton was shooting a movie there that day. When I arrived, Keaton was sitting in the back of a car. I took several of the movie stills I had brought from home to him. He signed them for me while describing the scenes in each one: 'Oh, that's the one from *Bedroom and Bath*.' It was an incredible day for me, one that [holds] lifelong memories." Keaton remained one of Maltin's favorite actors, along with some of the classic comedians like Laurel and Hardy and the Little Rascals gang. Later, other signed stills of classic movie stars joined his collection, including ones signed by Jimmy Stewart and Barbara Stanwyck.

Besides signed movie stills, Maltin has acquired several autographed books. While visiting Ginger Rogers, Maltin spotted a book on her shelf that was of new interest to him, "juvenile books from the '40s and '50s." When he pointed it out to her, she said, "Did you know my mother wrote that?" It was titled *Ginger Rogers and the Riddle of the Scarlet Cloak*, by Lela Rogers. According to Maltin, "I later found a copy and mailed it to her. She signed it for me, which I thought was really nice. Afterwards, I did the same thing with books about Gene Autry, Jane Withers, Roy Rogers, and others."

As far as displaying his collection, Maltin doesn't view them on a daily basis. His stills are categorized in files, and his books rest on the shelves of his bookcases at home. And, although Maltin has written books on Disney, he doesn't collect Disney memorabilia but has decided to stick with what he loves best. "I collect because I love it, not because of its value. Some of my favorite pieces are offbeat. That's what appeals to me, not the monetary value of them."

Maltin ended our conversation with an explanation of why he loves working on the television show that has made him a household name, though he sounds as if he may be talking about his quest for another movie still: "There is always an adventure."

Ginger Rogers and the Riddle of the Scarlet Cloak, a particularly special memento in Maltin's collection. *(Courtesy Leonard Maltin)*

Thanks to a popular television show and a string of hit singles, singer Barbara Mandrell was one of the biggest female stars in country music in the late 1970s and early 1980s. "I collect autographed books," Barbara told me. "I started collecting them about eighteen years ago." Barbara explained how she began collecting books: "It just sort of happened. I was excited to receive an autographed book but I can't remember who I got that first one from. From there I started accumulating more and more." Barbara said there isn't one type of book she collects and that she has a wide variety of titles in her collection.

Celebrities such as Erma Bombeck, Howard Cosell, and George Burns wrote several of the books in Barbara's collection. "I think Louise [Mandrell, Barbara's sister] got me the autographed book from George Burns because she worked with him," stated Barbara. "I'm blessed and happy to have some special books like Tammy Wynette's book, Jerry Clower, Minnie Pearl, people who have passed on. They are special to me. I also have Margaret Thatcher's *The Downing Street Years,* which was a gift."

Other books in Barbara's collection include those of famous writers. "I have a leather-bound full

collection of Louis L'Amour and he wrote sweet things to me. One book I have came from Bette Davis. It was signed, 'Hello to Barbara Mandrell, Enjoy hearing you, Bette Davis.' I guess if I had to pick a favorite it would be one from Dr. Billy Graham because it means a lot to me. And *The Hiding Place* by Corrie Ten Boom. It is a true story and it's a great book."

Barbara says she doesn't read all of the books she gets but states that she has great admiration for writers. "I treasure all of them— it sounds corny but be it fiction or nonfiction it's still a part of the writer. It's hard work."

Of Barbara's three-hundred-plus books, one that is very special is a book by Katherine Hepburn. "She never signs her books but she signed one for me and she wrote a little note in it for me." No telling what future additions may be in store for this collector.

Autographed books like those that may be in Barbara Mandrell's library.

Top: Barbara Mandrell *(Courtesy Barbara Mandrell)*

Talented singer and sister to Barbara Mandrell, entertainer Louise has been a collector for many years. "I collect hearts as well as Lladro figurines. I used to collect Shirley Temple memorabilia, and my favorite piece was a book that Shirley had signed for me. She told me that she rarely signs anything, so it was very special. When I was having a charity event at my home, someone stole the book. Since I've been blessed with my daughter, I no longer collect Shirley Temple memorabilia. She's my little Shirley Temple now!"

Louise has a collection that she passes along to others. "I will receive a heart from a friend. It may be crystal or porcelain or made out of another material, and then, after awhile, I'll pass that piece on to another friend of mine. One time a friend gave me a heart and I didn't have one to give back. So I drew a picture of a heart and signed it and gave it to her. Hearts are a fun thing to collect, and it's also fun to give them away to others."

One of Louise's favorite collections is plates. "I've been collecting them for years. I had a case made in my home in Nashville to display them. There isn't any particular kind that I like. It just depends what I'm drawn to. Many are given to me as gifts now that people know I have a collection of them."

DID YOU KNOW?

Actor John Larroquette hosts the A&E program *The Incurable Collector*. It appears that Larroquette is also a collector himself, acquiring first-edition books.

Top: Louise Mandrell *(Courtesy Louise Mandrell)*

Louise Mandrell with part of her plate collection. *(Courtesy Louise Mandrell)*

Born June 30, 1957, Sterling Marlin grew up around racecars. His dad, Coo Coo Marlin, was also a racecar driver. "I've been around racecars since I was in diapers," Sterling told me from his Columbia, Tennessee, home. Sterling made his Winston Cup debut in 1976, replacing his father after a crash hurt Coo Coo's shoulder. Since then, driving for Chip Ganassi Racing with Felix Sabates in his #40 car, he has earned ten victories, including two Daytona 500 victories in 1994-95 and Winston Open wins in 1988-89 and 1993.

Sterling's mind is not always on racing, however. Married to wife Paula, they share their home with their two children, Steadman and Sutherlin, but one room is just for Sterling. It's his "Civil War" room. As you enter the room there is a life-size painting of Sterling in a Civil War uniform gracing the wall. "I thought it would be fun to put that there," Sterling said with a smile.

Growing up in Columbia, Sterling has been able to accumulate many items to add to his collection of Civil War memorabilia. "We'll go hunting down by the old tracks," said Sterling. "I've found all kinds of things there, bullets, pieces of belts, even my favorite item, the top off a flag that went into battle." As items are found they seem to find their place in his Civil War room. Walls are lined with photos and memorabilia while the glass-top coffee table in the center of the room stays filled with many of his favorite items.

The Civil War era is very real to Sterling. "My great-great-great-granddaddy fought in the war. His name was William Joseph Marlin. He had three brothers and they all lived through the war and into their nineties. I have the papers that he used to travel with during the war." According to Sterling, "I've always been interested in the Civil War era. Ever since grammar school, because so much of the history happened around here. My mom used to talk about it all the time. I started hunting about 1990. I'll look around here and Richmond and different areas. I'll go out with a metal detector to find things and I've found buttons off uniforms, pieces of a harmonica; it's like a scavenger hunt. The railroad was built here in 1860 and the war started in 1861. I've got pictures of troops sitting on the trusses. They would guard the trusses to keep the enemy from coming and burning it."

While Sterling acquired many pieces by going out and hunting them for himself, several items in his collection are gifts from fans. "People have given me guns, swords, and various items. I have Custer's gun that was given to me. One time I was eating dinner at a steak house and someone came in with a cannon ball. 'I want you to have this,' he said, and handed it to me right there in the restaurant."

So what piece began Sterling's collection? "The first piece I got was a bullet. I also like to collect items associated with General Nathan Bedford Forrest. He started out as a private in the war and he worked up to a general. He was a self-made millionaire and would buy guns for his troops."

Other items in his collection include .69-caliber bullets that he found while searching the tracks. "I have found pieces of bridles; basically, pieces of everything they had during the war. My favorite piece is a flagstaff off a battle flag. It is the rarest piece I have. They would use it when they went into battle. I also have Confederate money a fan sent me and books on the Civil War that tell the history."

Though he still holds a love for collecting, racing has kept Sterling very busy. "I haven't had time to look for things like I used to and items are getting harder to find. If you have anything, you should hang on to it."

With his extensive collection there is still something Sterling would like to have. "A belt buckle," said Sterling. "I have one but I'd like to go out and find one myself. I think that would be exciting."

Top: Sterling Marlin poses with his race car. *(Courtesy Sterling Marlin and Chip Ganassi Racing with Felix Sabates)*

Top Center: Sterling with some of his Civil War figurines.

Actress and producer Demi Moore loves vintage clothing by various designers. Her favorite place to find them is at Lily et Cie in L.A., where she travels to pick up the newest finds.

Of course, as many people know, Moore's main collection is dolls. Her travels both in the U.S. and abroad have offered opportunities for Moore to pick up dolls from throughout the world. Did you know that a doll made in the likeness of Moore, wearing a navy, silk gown identical to the one she wore to the 1997 Emmy Awards, sold at auction for nineteen thousand dollars? The doll was designed by Patricia Chan, sculpted by Hussein Abbo, and adorned with twenty-five thousand handset Austrian crystal beads. The original dress was a vintage piece designed by Norman Norell, an American ready-to-wear designer whose career began in Hollywood in the '20s and lasted nearly fifty years.

The star of such films as *Ghost* and *Striptease,* Moore is an avid collector, and with the paychecks she receives for her film work, she can afford it. While on a trip to New Mexico, Moore stopped in a little antique store called the Dusty Attic. She reportedly walked out with tons of 1950s glassware and vintage mink stoles. In a story published in *People* magazine, Moore was reportedly buying them as gifts. It appears she likes sharing collectibles with her friends as well.

I'm sure the love of collecting has extended to her daughters, Rumer, Scout, and Tallulah. After all, don't all girls love dolls? Demi reportedly has so many dolls in her collection that they're kept in their own full-size Victorian house. The pastel-yellow home located in downtown Hailey, Idaho, has big picture windows with lead glass doors and seems the ideal setting for the collectible beauties. The house has been called a "doll collector's dream house." Reportedly, there are close to two thousand dolls in her collection, and they share the home with the girls' nanny. Now that's a lot of dolls!

Moore has said that there is no particular kind of doll she likes, but that she loves all dolls. She's been known to frequent Toy Fair, usually wearing no makeup so as not to stand out in the crowd. The annual New York trade show introduces the new lines of dolls for the upcoming year.

When I ran into actress and children's-book illustrator Jamie Lee Curtis in Chicago, I showed her a copy of one of the doll books I had written and the first thing she said to me was, "Has Demi Moore seen this?" It appears that Moore's collecting passion is no secret.

Moore's drive as an actor is equaled by her drive as a collector. Though known for buying vintage items (she recently purchased a telephone-shaped vintage handbag from the 1909 Company in New York), Moore is known to most in the collecting world as an avid fancier of beautiful dolls.

Top: Demi Moore is wearing the blue beaded gown that was re-created in doll form for a charity auction. *(Courtesy Shooting Stars)*

Dolls like those that Demi adores. *(Courtesy McMaster's/Harris)*

Rosie O'Donnell is an actress, comedienne, and collector. Those who tuned in to her daily talk show, *The Rosie O'Donnell Show*, could see happy-meal toys and memorabilia covering her desk. Her office may look more like a McDonald's restaurant than an office, with happy-meal toys abounding there as well: the 101 Dalmatians collection (yes, all 101), the Flintstones, you name it and O'Donnell probably has it in her collection. In an interview, O'Donnell told *Hot Toys Magazine,* "I started going to McDonald's every week [trying to get the entire collection of 101 Dalmatians]. When McDonald's heard I collect them, they sent me all of the 101 Dalmatians. Although that ruins it in some capacity, I have to say the level of joy I felt when I held all 101 in my hands is sort of indescribable." She has been called "a toy fanatic" and "a very active collector"—both titles fit her to a tee.

O'Donnell's Manhattan apartment boasts a wall of built-in shelves to hold part of her enormous toy collection. McDonald's happy-meal toys take center stage, with over twenty-five hundred pieces in her collection. Rosie started collecting happy-meal toys in the mid-1980s while touring the country as a stand-up comic. In an interview with *People* magazine, Rosie said, "They remind me of my childhood." McDonald's has since begun sending Rosie new releases as soon as they are available.

O'Donnell has other collections as well. Close behind on her list of favorite things are her dolls, which include a 1960 Chatty Cathy, a Kitty Carry-All from the *Brady Bunch* television series (given to her by Maureen McCormick, who played Marcia), and a Mrs. Beasley doll from the 1960s television series *Family Affair.* O'Donnell has stated she loves the toys that fans have sent to her, adding to her massive collection. In addition to these collections, Rosie acquires figures based on television shows, such as *Star Trek* and *I Dream of Jeannie.* She even has a few Mr. Potato Heads sitting around.

Guests of O'Donnell's show also helped her add to her collection. When Lucy Lawless appeared on the show, Rosie did the opposite and handed her a Xena doll that the actress had never seen before.

Now, O'Donnell has become a collectible herself! There are several dolls that have been made in her

likeness, including a Rosie Barbie by Mattel and a cloth doll that says various phrases when you squeeze her, including "What a cutie patootie!" In 1994, Mattel produced a Betty Rubble figure made in O'Donnell's likeness, from the film *The Flintstones.*

Rosie has been called "Queen of Nice" by *Newsweek; Ladies Home Journal* dubbed her one of the most "fascinating women of the year." Perhaps, we should add another title: "Ultimate Collector."

Top: Rosie O'Donnell *(AP Photo)*

Bottom: Rosie loves to collect McDonald's toys.

"I love butterflies because they are free and beautiful," stated actress, singer, writer, and composer Dolly Parton. A native of Sevier County, Tennessee, Parton began her singing career by performing with Porter Wagoner. Wagoner was looking for a singer to replace his previous singing partner on his syndicated television show. Parton signed on in 1967 and remained with the show until 1974. In 1968, she joined RCA Records, and the following year, she became a member of the Grand Ole Opry. In addition to now owning her own record label and television/film production company, Parton flosses acting credentials that include starring in such blockbuster movies as *Steel Magnolias* and *The Best Little Whorehouse in Texas.*

When I asked Dolly why she started collecting butterflies, she told me, "Well, I always loved butterflies. My mama said I was always so tricky. I guess it was the colors in them, 'cause I love loud colors. And when I was little, she said I used to always follow these butterflies around, hoppin' around the flowers, and I used to always get lost, and she'd always have to come out and find me. I wasn't afraid of them, you know, like some bugs. But they were just so gentle and colorful and spiritual. And that just kind of became my little emblem 'cause I feel sort of like that. I ain't out to hurt nobody, but I do want to hop from one thing to another."

Parton collects butterflies, that is, anything with a butterfly on it. She owns a chair shaped like a butterfly, and the museum at her Dollywood theme park, the Chasing Rainbow Museum, displays a multitude of butterfly-related items, including jewelry, pillows, and more. In fact, if you walk through the park, you will see butterflies everywhere. They are

on the ends of lampposts and engraved into the ground. The theme park's rollercoaster ride, the Tennessee Tornado, has a section that Parton calls "the iron butterfly." Butterflies are also in the museum of mementos from her childhood, along with a couple of her prized possessions—a corncob doll she calls Tassel Top, which she said her mother made, and a coat of many colors, which was the inspiration of the song of the same name. "Things in the museum are from my life, and they are special to me," said Parton. On the park grounds, you can see a replica of the two-room home that Parton shared with her eleven brothers and sisters. But butterflies are what make this country girl smile. She even wrote a song entitled "Love is Like a Butterfly," with lyrics that say, "Love is like a butterfly, a rare and gentle thing."

Many of the butterfly items in Parton's collection were sent from fans. A large number of butterfly pins line one of the drawers in the museum. They lay alongside butterfly necklaces and various other pieces of butterfly jewelry. The assortment of items in Parton's collection is as diverse as the many talents of this amazing lady.

Top: Dolly Parton *(Courtesy Dollywood Publicity)*

A picture of the floor of Dolly's museum at Dollywood and outside of one of the buildings at Dollywood. The park has butterfly images throughout.

Actress and singer Debbie Reynolds has starred in numerous motion pictures, Broadway shows, and television series. Her recordings of "Abba Dabba Honeymoon" (from *Two Weeks with Love*) and "Tammy" both sold more than a million copies. Reynolds is also major collector of movie memorabilia. She is responsible for saving some part of the history of cinema and preserving an incredible collection of clothing and memorabilia.

Since the late 1960s, Reynolds has also been involved in collecting and preserving the memorabilia from Hollywood's first half-century of filmmaking. Reynolds was responsible for acquiring thousands of props, costumes, and mementos of the Hollywood studios and their biggest stars. In 1993, her longtime dream of preserving Hollywood memorabilia came to life with the opening of the Debbie Reynolds Hollywood Hotel and Movie Museum in Las Vegas. The museum housed a multitude of artifacts that movie buffs would drool over. Reynolds' collection is considered the largest personally owned collection of Hollywood memorabilia. In 1997 the Debbie Reynolds Hotel and Casino filed for Chapter 11 bankruptcy, but the hotel remained open for a time and was a showcase for her glitzy collection, boasting over three thousand costumes and thirty-six thousand square feet of props. The collection is valued at over thirty million dollars. Among the items from her collection are Elizabeth Taylor's headdress from the film *Cleopatra* (which sold at auction) and Judy Garland's pinafore dress from *The Wizard of Oz*.

The collection will be displayed in Pigeon Forge, Tennessee, in a new museum so this wonderful and exceptional collection will be available for public viewing. It's a variety that will probably not be equaled anytime soon.

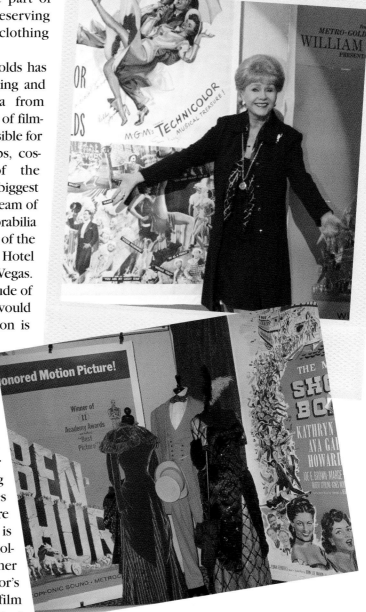

Top: Debbie Reynolds (*Courtesy Debbie Reynolds*)

Bottom: A small sampling of the wealth of movie memorabilia Debbie Reynolds has collected. (*Courtesy Debbie Reynolds*)

Caroline Rhea collects couches. Yes, couches. "I know it's an unusual thing to collect," stated Rhea. One piece in her collection is actually a miniature doll couch given to her as a gift. "I also collect small ceramic pieces," she explained.

Rhea is widely known as the person who replaced Rosie O'Donnell to create her own talk show, *The Caroline Rhea Show,* which ended in 2003. Many know her as a regular on *Hollywood Squares* and as Aunt Hilda on the WB's *Sabrina, the Teenage Witch.* "I know people think, 'Where [does she] put them?'" Rhea says, referring to her couch collection. "However, I own homes in different areas, so I really do have space for them."

DID YOU KNOW?

Producer Joel Silver (*Die Hard, Predators 1 and 2, Lethal Weapon*) says he enjoys arts and crafts. "I don't make art, I buy it," Silver told *Art & Antique.* His favorite artist is Frank Lloyd Wright. He has bought and renovated Wright's homes, including the Storer house in Hollywood Hills and South Carolina's Auldbrass plantation.

Caroline Rhea

A miniature couch given to Caroline as a gift.

Richard Simmons is a huge doll collector. He just loves them—but not any doll. Richard prefers artist dolls. What's an artist doll? It's a creation by a doll artist, often one of a kind.

Simmons told me one of his sixth-grade memories. This was, perhaps, his first doll purchase: "There was a very poor girl who sat across from me [in class], and her parents were divorced, and people made fun of her. No one would let her play with their dolls. It was Christmas time, and my father took me shopping. I told him instead of buying me a gift I wanted to buy a doll for a girl in my class who had nothing. My father walked up to a clerk and asked which was the prettiest doll they had. I was shocked because my father was a little frugal. Out from behind the counter, this lady brought out a Barbie doll in the most elaborate wedding gown I had ever seen. Without hesitation, my father said, 'Wrap it up.'

"The next day at school, everyone opened a package underneath the tree—you know how you pick names from a hat and you had to buy one of your classmates a present. I had purposely picked this girl's name. I got to school early that day and put the package under the tree with the others. I made a card for her and wrote her name in Elmer's glue and put glitter all over the top. When it was time, after lunch, everyone ran to the tree to find their package. Sarah

Richard Simmons *(Courtesy Richard Simmons)*

was quite surprised to see that hers was the biggest package, with the biggest bow and a glittered card.

As all the other kids were ripping their paper from their packages, Sarah quietly opened her package at her desk. I watched every movement she made and watched her eyes as she opened this box to see this magnificent Barbie. Tears ran down her face as she held the doll so tightly. I guess that began my love of dolls. They bring me joy and love, and firsthand, I saw that a doll can spread a spell of love to all."

Growing up in the colorful New Orleans area, Simmons was constantly surrounded by art and eye-catching things. He once worked in a wax museum and there developed a love for life-sized figures. Later, while studying in Italy, he adopted Michelangelo as his favorite artist. With his background in fashion illustration and design, he moved to New York City in the 1960s. He did a variety of things before becoming one of the most loved fitness gurus today (with his television shows, video workouts, and meal plans). Simmons moved to Beverly Hills, where one of his loved collections, art glass sculptures from the worlds top glass artists, was destroyed in the 1994 Northridge earthquake. A friend gave him a one-of-a-kind artist doll to make him feel better, and from that, his doll-collecting days began.

But dolls are not the only things that Simmons collects. He told me he also has quite a collection of pigs and dalmatians. Though the foyer of his beautiful and relaxing home is filled with wonderful figures of dolls, each with their own pedestal, collections of dalmatians, pigs, and angels all have their special place in Simmons' home and in his heart. "I collect contemporary dolls from all over the world, pigs, angels, and Dalmatian collectibles," stated Richard.

The diet and fitness guru of this century began collecting at a young age. "Since I was overweight as a child, I began collecting pigs, because I thought they were relatives," he joked. Simmons' pigs are created in many different materials, but the one piece that stands out is of the cloth variety. He explains, "Some lady sent me a six-foot cloth pig. I kept it in the passenger seat of my car. A police car pulled me over because he just couldn't believe what he was seeing."

Dalmatians are another of Simmons' loves. He has not only the collectible assortment, but also some of the live ones. A photograph taken of him for *McCall's* shows Richard sitting on a dalmatian-spotted couch with three of his pet dogs.

Richard Simmons' massive collection of dolls. *(Courtesy Richard Simmons)*

Behind is an array of dalmatian dogs made of ceramic, plaster, and glass. They range in size from a couple of inches to two feet high. Talk about spots before your eyes! It was hard to tell where one dalmatian stopped and the other started.

When asked why he started collecting, Simmons responded, "Collections are created to surround someone and make them smile. My parents collected many things, and I followed in their footsteps." His love for dolls is so strong that he introduced a line of dolls for the L. L. Knickerbocker Company. After years of working to reproduce the works of some of his favorite doll artists, this line, Collection of the Masters, was presented to the public. To Simmons, dolls are joy, and he likes to share that joy. He has been known to accomplish this by giving dolls away to others. In a *DollReader* interview, he explains, "There are so many unhappy people in the world, that I truly believe that when they have some things around that make them smile, and that give them a happy memory, then you've served a lot of different purposes. And that makes my day."

Barbra Streisand is a multitalented entertainer, actress, and singer. She also has an incredible collection of various items, including arts-and-crafts pieces and art-deco items. She has amassed a world-class collection of twentieth-century decorative art and design, a collection she has accumulated for over thirty years. Streisand is probably one of the most advanced celebrity collectors around, with a wide assortment of collectibles under her ownership.

In 1999, Christie's of New York auctioned off many of Streisand's pieces. Nancy McClelland of Christie's stated about the auction, "Ms. Streisand's enormous fame will no doubt contribute to the excitement with which collectors all over the world will greet this sale. More importantly, serious collectors will relish the unexpected opportunity to acquire great examples from her collection." In the spring of 1994, Christie's also sold a collection of Art Nouveau and art-deco pieces belonging to Streisand.

Barbra Streisand shown here with a Golden Globe. It appears Barbra also collects awards. (AP Photo)

McClelland, speaking of Streisand's Stickley furniture collection, explained, "This is even more a connoisseur's collection than the one Christie's offered before. Each piece has been carefully researched and selected for its design and craftsmanship." Christie's auction included some notable pieces by Gustav Stickley and L. & J. G. Stickley. Gustav Stickley was the leading exponent of the arts-and-crafts style in the United States, and the recent arts-and-crafts movement has made Stickley furniture very popular with collectors. A highlight of Streisand's collection was a 1902 sideboard, originally made for Stickley's own home in Syracuse

and estimated to sell between three hundred thousand and four hundred thousand dollars. Streisand purchased the cabinet at Christie's in December 1988. A pair of corner cabinets that Streisand bought at another Christie's auction in 1989 was offered for a presale estimate of between twenty-six thousand and thirty-four thousand dollars each.

In addition to pieces by Stickley, pieces by Frank Lloyd Wright, Charles Rennie Mackintosh, and Dirk van Erp make up Streisand's collection. Frank Lloyd Wright pieces that sold included a library table (estimate: one hundred thousand to one hundred fifty thousand dollars), a pair of oak high-back side chairs (estimate: fifty thousand to seventy thousand dollars each), an oak console table (estimate: sixty thousand to eighty thousand dollars), and an oak reclining chair (estimate: forty thousand to sixty thousand dollars). Part of Streisand's other collections—pieces by Hector Guimard, Charles Rennie Mackintosh, and Emile Gallé—were also sold, though Streisand kept some of her favorite pieces for her own collection.

Streisand also collects lamps and ceramics, many by Tiffany. Many of these types of items were sold at the Christie's auction—perhaps, a way to thin out her collection. One "Dragonfly" shade on a turtle-back-tiled mosaic glass and bronze base was estimated to sell for $180,000 to $240,000. Streisand also has a love of fine pottery, evident from her pieces by William Grueby, which she was parting with at the auction. Grueby vases were commissioned by

Tiffany to be used as lamp bases surmounted with glass shades. These were estimated at the twenty-thousand-to-thirty-thousand-dollar mark.

Several other pieces of Streisand's personal property were also put up for sale, including a Lalique grey vase, with an estimate of four thousand to six thousand dollars, and several pieces of Tiffany glass, Pata-de-Verre art glass by Almeric Walter, and Argy Rousseau and Galle glass vases.

A big fan of designer Donna Karan, Streisand also collects vintage clothing. However, even some of these pieces managed to make it out of her closet and to the auction floor. An array of vintage handbags, vintage shoes, hats, and designer clothing by Donna Karan, Calvin Klein, Jean Muir, Jil Sander, and Giorgio Armani sold for just a few hundreds of dollars to up in the thousands of dollars.

As it turned out, the collection, or what Streisand was willing to part with, sold for $32,765,406, setting many world records. The highlight was the Tiffany "Magnolia" floor lamp, which sold for $1,762,500.

Recently some of her perfume bottles were sold on eBay, including a rare metal wood-and-glass enameled Mellier Perfume Display. It was part of her personal collection of Art Nouveau and art deco collections.

These Art Deco perfume bottles are some of the items that have found there way into Barbra's collection. *(Courtesy Starwares Collectibles)*

Sally Struthers told *Collectibles Illustrated* magazine, "I think collecting is a fun and healthy thing for people to do. It's creative to decide what you want to collect and then become involved with it. You may not be athletic enough to ski or ride a motorcycle, but you can still have a lot of fun collecting."

Struthers is best known for her role as Gloria on the hit television series *All in the Family.* Currently, she is acting in the theatre and television and has worked for a cause that is very dear to her, Save the Children, an organization founded to help young children have a chance for a safe, healthy, and happy childhood.

When not working on her many projects, Struthers loves to collect. Though her collecting has slowed dramatically in the last few years, at one time, she was anything but a lightweight in the collecting field.

Cats were Struthers' biggest acquisition, and her collection included items ranging from cat dolls and figurines to feline prints and posters. From over a decade of collecting cat paraphernalia, she had cats of every shape, size, and description imaginable. Items included cat doorstops, bowls, planters, cookie jars, boxes, pictures, and even a cat lamp.

In Struthers' interview with *Collectibles Illustrated,* she said, "My most unusual cat find occurred when I went to a sale held by the owner of a beauty shop. He was moving to a different house and had decided to sell some personal artifacts. The first thing I saw were two ancient canvas carnival cats like those people attempt to knock

over with baseballs in order to win a prize. I got them both for five dollars." She continued, "Your collections can occupy you at the strangest times. You can be out somewhere at a garage sale or in a store and see something that catches your fancy and would look lovely in your collection. I have several things I look for and my eye seems to go right to them if they are around. It's a way of gifting yourself with a nice little keepsake. Or, when someone wants to give you a gift, they should know what you like."

Besides cats, Struthers has found joy in collecting other items, including small boxes, teddy bears, antique perfume bottles, thimbles, and blackiana.

In a story about Struthers' collections, she described her childhood collection. Her first collection of stuffed animals disappeared one day. Later that day, she discovered that her mother had given nearly all her stuffed animals to a local orphanage. Though upset at the time, the memory stayed with her. This, in some part, may have set Sally on the path of helping other children, a responsibility she learned from her mother. No matter how big your collections may be, the pleasure of sharing them with others can be as fulfilling as keeping it yourself. According to Struthers, "I guess you could say that my first collection was dispersed for a very good reason."

Top: Sally Struthers *(Courtesy Sally Struthers)*

Bottom: Struthers with one of her stuffed cats.

Want to play? That may be a question you'd like to ask Quentin Tarantino. Rumor has it that this director, producer, actor, and screenwriter likes to play and collect games, specifically, board games!

JUICY TIDBIT!

A 1933 twenty-dollar gold piece was on display at the Federal Reserve Bank in New York. Once owned by King Faruk, the last reigning king of Egypt and an avid collector, the piece is the only one of its kind legally in private hands. The coin was designed by Augustus Saint-Gaudens. An anonymous bidder bought it at auction in July 2002 for $7.59 million. It's considered the world's most valuable coin.

Writer/director/actor Quentin Tarantino may be thinking of his next move. *(AP Photo)*

Tarantino has the fun hobby of collecting board games.

Alan Thicke, the former star of the hit television show *Growing Pains,* is known to many of us as Jason Seaver. But this fine actor, writer, and author is also a collector. He began his career by writing and has won five of his seven Emmy nominations for the craft. When not writing, acting, or working on a variety of other projects, Thicke loves to collect hockey memorabilia. We spoke about some of his collecting loves. Alan decided it might be best to tell readers about his collecting hobby in his own words. Enjoy.

> Let the others collect all their Oscars,
> their Emmys and Grammys, that's wise.
> Some stars collect girlfriends and autos;
> Some save all their past DUIs.
> My hobby is truly Canadian;
> It's common to many Canucks.
> I gather whatever I can
> That relates to the great sport of pucks.
> Score sheets and sticks from the great one
> Appear at the top of my list.
> There's Gretzky, Lemieux, Orr, and Howe, too—
> There aren't many players I've missed.
> Beyond that, I did save one ticket,
> A stub not related to pucks,
> The Beatles tour back in the '60s.
> The price?
> Just a measly five bucks!

The above poem tells you a bit about Thicke and his collection, but let me share more. "A sports groupie" is how he describes himself. Thicke grew up with a love for hockey and collecting. But he is not your typical collector. Most collectors buy things only to trade or sell them later or to "set them aside" for "that certain day." Alan's reasons for collecting are much more personal. "I have items from many different sports, but my main collection is hockey. I still play once a week. From other sports, I have a Larry Bird basketball signed, baseballs signed by . . . MVP[s] from both leagues, Larry Walker and Ken Griffey, Jr. I was on tour with the musical *Chicago,* so I got to throw out the first pitch at some major league games while traveling and that gave me the opportunity to collect many

things. I've got a football signed by five Heisman trophy winners, including Tony Dorsett, George Rogers, and Johnny Rodgers. The majority of my collection has to do with hockey. In fact, some of my collection is now second generation. My boys have collected a few things, including Carter. He has a pair of autographed baby skates from hall-of-famer Rod Gilbert of the Rangers; he has a Boston Bruins #4 Bobby Orr sweater he got for his birthday, autographed and given to him by Bobby. He also got a couple of really nice personalized items from Chris Everett and Jack Nicklaus, and a Bret Favre autographed football. My two older sons have Wayne Gretzky hockey sticks." Thicke has been a friend of Gretzky's for years and has called him the "puck god."

When asked how long he has been collecting sports memorabilia, Thicke said, "Probably since I was eleven. In fact, my first autograph book was filled with signatures from the Hamilton Tiger Cats football team from the Canadian league. My connection there was my idol, a kicker named Cal Fraser. He has since passed away. We had kept in touch all those years. He was a world-class kicker with the Tiger Cats. That first autograph spawned a relationship that lasted forty years

Alan Thicke *(Courtesy Alan Thicke)*

until his death. . . . He was an usher at my first wedding. That all started from an autograph at age eleven."

Thicke said some of his favorite pieces include one of only two original copies of the official NHL score sheet from the game in which Wayne Gretzky broke Gordie Howe's record for total career points. "It's signed by Wayne and Gordie," said Thicke. "I have an office in my house where I display many of the pieces from my collection."

Thicke told me about an unusual collectible he acquired. "I got a very nice letter. It was sent to me by Pete Rose and postmarked from jail. He was incarcerated in Marion County for his gambling problems. This was during the time that *Growing Pains* was on television. The letter said that I was a good role model for career rehabilitation. Having been cancelled on *The Thicke of the Night,* and then the next year I was on *Growing Pains.* It was a lovely sentiment. I had never met him before that. I've run into him a couple of times, and he was very pleasant."

Thicke said he has several personal items in his collection. He states, "I have hockey sticks, sweaters, and memorabilia from some of my idols. They include hall-of-famers Mario Lemieux, Gordie Howe, Stanley

Mikita, Marcel Dionne and Phil Esposito."

Thicke says he doesn't buy anything in his collection. "I treasure the personal contact that affords me the opportunity to collect personalized things. I don't collect things to sell or trade them. It's purely for my own and my children's memorabilia." And while he doesn't have anything in the way of Michael Jordan memorabilia, he does have one special piece. "I do have a very special videotape of an occasion when we all played some golf and basketball together. They covered it for an NBA special. It included my son Robin, who was ten at the time. I have that bit of memorabilia on tape." According to Thicke, his collection is "private, it's personal, and it has a lot of fond memories."

Alan collects hockey memorabilia. Wayne Gretzky items are a personal favorite.

Actress Lea Thompson, who is best known for her role on *Caroline in the City* and the *Back to the Future* trilogy, loves to collect. Pottery, including Roseville, is one of her main loves. "I just love Roseville Pottery. When we were putting our bathroom together, I tried to duplicate the colors of the Roseville Pottery with the tiles, but it was just too hard. The glazes they used then are just too hard to duplicate today." Instead, she settled on the 1930s look for her bathroom, which has a Spanish feel and large blue tiles in the center with darker ones around the edges. "I put my Roseville pieces that have the blue tones [cobalt] in the bathroom. They are lined on shelves on both sides of the bathtub."

Thompson's home is filled with stained-glass windows, many of which her mother designed, and unique items like an antique carousel horse. Yet, many of the collectibles in Thompson's home have a more useful purpose. "I collect dishes from the '50s, and I use them all the time. In fact, during one of our chats, I was able to secure some dishes in the Poppy trail California ivy pattern while on eBay. I'm not very computer literate," Thompson admits. "Most of what I find is from flea markets, antique shows, and garage sales." Her home, a seven-thousand-square-foot Los Angeles getaway with seven acres, gives her lots of room to store her collectibles. "My kitchen is filled with dishes from the '50s," she described. "They are functional and pretty at the same time. The glass cabinets give open view to the assortment of dishes to be had."

Thompson spends her free time with her husband, director Howard Deutch (*Grumpier Old Men* and *The Odd Couple II*), and her daughters, Maddelyn and Zoey. "The kids like Beanie Babies," Thompson admits. But she is the collecting leader in this household. "I love old teapots too. I have several of them lined up in my kitchen. I also love vintage clothing and old purses from the 1950s. They are fun to use and photographers love to take pictures of me with them." Antiques are found throughout her home, and there are some with a mod flair, like the 1960s chandeliers that hang in the kitchen, complete with a flower motif. "I had a really hard time finding all the lighting I wanted for the house," stated Thompson. "I still don't really have everything I want. One light I found while looking through an old second-hand store." In the face of all of Thompson's collectibles, her husband doesn't come out empty handed. The house has a library that includes not only pieces of Thompson's pottery, but also shelves of books for hubby to read in his spare time.

To finish off her array of collectibles, Thompson has several oil paintings along with prints by Louis Icart and various art-deco statuettes of dancers. "I've been a dancer all my life, starting with ballet as a little girl, and I just love the statuettes of the dancers," stated Thompson. "Collecting is something I really enjoy."

Top: Lea Thompson *(AP Photo)*

Bottom: Lea loves Roseville Pottery.

John Travolta is an all-around actor, beginning his career as Vinnie Barbarino on the hit television show *Welcome Back, Kotter* then following in films like *Saturday Night Fever,* which made him a '70s sex symbol. After the film *Pulp Fiction* was released, there was new interest in this experienced actor. His career catapulted, making Travolta one of the biggest stars today, with films like *Swordfish, The General's Daughter,* and *Phenomenon.*

Travolta loves to fly. He even wrote a book, *Propeller One-Way Night Coach,* about a young boy's first flight. Travolta, who grew up in New Jersey, said, "Our home was under La Guardia airport's flight pattern. Planes would be at three thousand feet when they flew over." So, you could say Travolta grew up around airplanes. He collects items related to aviation, in particular, flight schedules, especially ones by TWA. "I collect them and study them. I like all kinds of airline and aircraft memorabilia. I started collecting when I was seven years old. My sister Ellen gave me my first schedule and old airline ticket." Travolta has been collecting for over four decades now, a long time for any collector.

So, if he has such a varied collection, what might be his favorite piece? Travolta told me, "It's a 1958 TWA schedule. It was for the longest propeller-airline trip in history. It was going from Los Angeles to London, nonstop for twenty-two hours. Then, from San Francisco to Paris, nonstop for twenty-two hours. My mother-in-law (from his marriage to actress Kelly Preston) was actually on that flight in 1958. She was on the Paris part of the flight."

While Travolta loves TWA memorabilia, he took to the skies as Qantas Airways' official ambassador at large. Travolta has his own private Boeing 707 (one of several planes he owns), an old Qantas jetliner he hoped to restore to its original 1960s state, complete with Qantas's classic colors. In fact, Qantas agreed to give Travolta's jet a fresh coat of paint in exchange for the actor hyping the airline. To prepare, Travolta took courses with Qantas and practiced on Boeing 747 simulators at the airplane manufacturer's Seattle

facility. After the finishing touches went on the plane, including the words "Jett Clipper Ella," after his children, Travolta took off for his round-the-world adventure, leaving from Los Angeles, with stops in Auckland, New Zealand, and the Australian cities of Sydney, Melbourne, and Perth. He was then off to Singapore, Hong Kong, Tokyo, London, Rome, Paris, and Frankfurt before landing safely in New York.

Other planes in Travolta's collection include a Gulfstream II, a Learjet 24B, and a civilian version of a two-seat Canadair CL-41G Tebuan military trainer. He began flying at a young age. He told *Professional Pilot,* "Every cent of my first paychecks went to flying lessons and I'd have done anything to be a part of aviation. I started acting early, but you never know what career is going to work out. I decided that if my acting career didn't work out, I'd find some way to become part of aviation."

Travolta has flown privately since 1978, and he earned his jet rating at age twenty-six. Travolta's paychecks went from paying for flying lessons to purchasing airplanes like a Jet Commander, Citation ISP, Jetstar, Citation II, Hawker IA, DC-3, and a Constellation.

As a collector, Travolta admires the era of the Pan Am Clippers and the early BOAC international services, when style and elegance were part of the flight. On board the N492JT, Travolta offers a silver-tray service with flowers, wine lists, and a cabin that converts into five berths. He considers many things before purchasing an aircraft, including required comfort level, operational factors, and reliability. And, while collecting the actual aircraft is fun, it's the hunt for the rare flight tables and memorabilia that keeps this collector on the lookout.

In addition to airplanes, Travolta also has a nice collection of antique cars.

Top: John Travolta in his airplane. *(Courtesy John Travolta)*

Bottom: This toy Alaska Airlines plane was a gift from the author to Travolta. It is a limited-edition die-cast plane from an aviation-memorabilia show.

Ivana Trump is used to living the high life. The former Mrs. Donald Trump, a businesswoman in her own right (she is also a published author), lives a plush life and loves to buy beautiful things. Trump told me that she collects many things, including chandeliers that hang around several rooms in her home. "I have many crystal chandeliers. The lights are so beautiful when they shine through the crystals." She also collects women's compacts and sits them around her home as unique and beautiful accessories. She said some of her favorites include compacts with faux jewels. "I love to actually use the products inside," she explained. Then she will display it along with other art pieces around her home. "I've been collecting for all my life. I have good memories of where and when I would find a special piece."

Pins are another collector's item that Trump rarely passes up. "I love unusual dress pins. My signature pin is a jeweled spider that I give to all of my closest friends."

Glass and crystal are both a love of Trump's. "I started collecting when I was in Czechoslovakia, and then, later, I would find things at auction houses or in Italy."

Trump said that some of her favorite pieces include Czech glasses and Murano chandeliers. The dining room where she holds her business meetings has a beautiful chandelier as its centerpiece. According to Trump, "Many of the pieces are so beautiful. The glasses for instance are hand-blown, edged, or hand-painted, or made over a flame." With numerous homes, Trump has room to collect many beautiful chandeliers, and the prices aren't as bad as one would think. In fact, many Murano chandeliers can be bought for just a couple of thousand dollars apiece, and for Trump, there is an abundance to be had.

Even daughter Ivanka has got into the collecting mode. She has a collection of antique pillboxes and fragrance bottles.

Top: Ivana Trump *(Courtesy Ivana Trump)*

Right: These chandeliers are examples of the sparkling items one might find in Ivana Trump's collection.

JOHN WALSH
BOXES, MOTORCYCLES, KNIVES, AND MAGNIFYING GLASSES

Talk-show host and child activist John Walsh, star of *America's Most Wanted,* said he collects knives, motorcycles, boxes, and magnifying glasses. "Many of the handles on old magnifying glasses are very unique. They are made out of many different materials, and I find them very interesting. The same is true with many old knives. I also have a large collection of boxes in many types of materials. I probably have about two hundred of them. I can't say I have a favorite. They are all unique in their own way. I really like them all."

DID YOU KNOW?
LeAnn Rimes is a young lady with a love for shoes. She has admitted to having over seventy-five pairs. One of her favorite designers is Steve Madden.

An antique knife and a magnifying glass found in Walsh's own collection.

Top: John Walsh *(Courtesy* Smoky Mountain Herald*)*

Bruce Williams *(Courtesy Bruce Williams)*

Walking around the home of talk-show host Bruce Williams (he has the second-highest-rated talk show in the country behind Rush Limbaugh), it is no secret that he is a collector. A large, life-size Pinocchio doll hangs from a corner in one room. One wall is lined with slot machines, a fun pastime for guests. Coins, while not out on display, are another of Williams' collecting passions. He took me aside to show me a variety of rare and unusual coins, which he had collected over the years. There is no rhyme or reason to Williams' collections. He collects what he likes. "I collect, without regard to cost. My 'stuff' that I have accumulated over the years is very eclectic, and value, as described by dollars, is meaningless," stated Williams. "As an example, I have a little bird which I paid eight cents for and is very dear to me, and also single coins, of which I have invested upwards of thirty thousand dollars

in. Very rarely will I dispose of anything. I collect things because I happen to like them. I have a very substantial accumulation of Disney items, from watches and other types of timepieces, statuary, and even a life-size Pinocchio puppet. I have the first parachute ring that I ever pulled, a great many wooden and other representatives of birds, given that most of my companies are named after birds. People in Alaska have been very generous with parts of woolly mammoths, statuary, and so forth."

There are several favorites in Williams' collections. "One of my favorite pieces is a highly polished brass piece about fifteen inches tall, with knobs on one end and full of holes. This brass piece was the filter on a sucker hose from a 1934 fire engine I acquired many years ago, for a play area for the children in the nursery school that I then owned. Ultimately, even a solid steel truck can't handle the onslaught of the children and it was junked. Thirty years later, I found it in the woods, with the sucker hose still strapped tightly on with the plastic straps that I had used three decades before. I sawed off the brass fitting, sent it out and had it cleaned with acid and polished, and it is now sitting in my Florida home. I suspect of all the things that I have ensconced, the Lladro, a couple of Ming pieces, etc., this is the most highly prized."

So you can see that price does not a prized collectible make.

Coins like those Williams may collect.

Actor, director, producer, and children's-book author Henry Winkler collects things that remind him of his past. "I collect hats and shirts from all the shows I've produced or have acted in. I also collect patches or pins of every place that I've been in the world. I attach them to this army-style khaki uniform shirt. It has every patch and pin of everywhere I've been. I also collect hats from way back. I have the hat that I worn in *Night Shift.* We went into a burger place, and they created their own logo and their own hat and I have that. I have hats from all the shows I've been on. The *Happy Days* cast used to have a baseball team, and we'd travel around to different cities playing. One time we were playing Tug McGraw, and he gave me his hat. It's a fun collection."

Henry Winkler *(Courtesy Henry Winkler)*

Henry Winkler loves pins from around the world.

Casino mogul Steve Wynn has been adding some delightful pieces to his massive art collection. The pieces were purchased to help decorate the Bellagio, the $1.6 billion casino-resort that he built. A report from TheStreet.com reported than Wynn and his company, Mirage Resorts, Inc., spent an astounding total of $285 million on art in an eighteen-month period. Wynn was hoping to attract the best of the tourists to his establishment.

Some of Wynn's purchases include Edgar Degas's pastel *Dancer Taking Her Bow* ($12 million), Pablo Picasso's 1956 oil on canvas *Seated Woman* ($1.6 Million), Alberto Giacometti's *Pointing Man* ($7.35 million), and an Henri Matisse still life ($4.6 million). Out of twelve paintings purchased, eleven were set for the Bellagio, while the Picasso was headed for Wynn's personal estate, an estate through which I'd love to take a tour!

Since that great undertaking Wynn has purchased the Desert Inn property, and the Wynn Las Vegas, previously planned to be named Le Reve after a Picasso painting, opened in spring 2005.

Steve Wynn with artwork from his collection. *(Courtesy Christine H. Wetzel,* Las Vegas Review-Journal*)*

DID YOU KNOW?

Actor and director Forest Whitaker knows his African roots. He is surrounded by a collection of African art at home. His living room is decorated with a mix of African masks and furniture.

This is a special tribute section for the millions of Americans who still read the magazines and books, listen to the albums, and watch the shows of these past collectors. Though they are no longer with us, their love of collecting and the joy they have brought to so many will always remain.

Morey Amsterdam was known to many of us as the fun-loving Buddy Sorrell on *The Dick Van Dyke Show.* The show, deemed a television classic, ran from October 1961 until June 1966. Through syndication, *The Dick Van Dick Show* has been seen by millions of people in every age group. That's what makes Amsterdam's face so familiar to us.

His love of collecting came from his real-life love, playing the cello. Amsterdam was raised to be a concert cellist. His father was concertmaster of the San Francisco Symphony Orchestra for thirty-five years, and it was expected that Amsterdam would also be involved in music. He told *Collectibles Illustrated,* "In real life and in miniature, cello players are hard to find." There are about twenty-five violin players to every cello player.

His collection featured figures of many sizes and descriptions. Many were made of porcelain and came from countries like Spain, Ireland, and Italy, with some of the pieces dating back over one hundred years. One of his most unusual figures was made up of silverware, including a spoon, fork, and cake server. Amsterdam told *Collectibles Illustrated,* "In Hong Kong where I expected to find a lot of cello players, I never found one. In China I saw people buying real cellos, but saw no cello artwork." One of Amsterdam's favorite pieces was a cello player with his face made up like a clown.

His wife, Kay Amsterdam, who has an interior-design business in Beverly Hills, told me, "I collected the cellos with Morey, as Morey played cellos and so often used them in his act. Cellos are very hard to find. They often mix up cellos with bass players." Amsterdam collected cellos more for his wife, Kay, than for himself.

Amsterdam's love for acting, music, and cellos will be remembered always.

Morey Amsterdam and his cello *(Courtesy Ralph Merlino)*

Lucille Ball. The name conjures the image of a beautiful woman with bright-red hair and more often than not will bring a smile to your face. She was the greatest comic in the history of television. Bob Hope was quoted as saying, "She brought more laughs to the world than anyone ever to appear on television." She began her career, which spanned fifty years, as a bleached-blonde model who dabbled in acting. We all knew her as Lucy Ricardo, who made her debut in October 1951 on the hit television show *I Love Lucy.*

Millions would tune in to watch her with husband Ricky and sidekicks Ethel and Fred. Ball went on to form her own production company, Desilu, with her husband, Desi, and produced such hits as *Star Trek* and *The Untouchables.*

Though most people never knew about her passion for collecting, it would become apparent with her passing. No matter what you do during your life, it seems you are able to capture part of it in pictures and videos. Lucy took that idea and ran with it. The results were astounding. Lucie Arnaz, daughter of the legendary television comedienne, was quoted in an interview in *Collecting Online,* "My mother was a collector of amazing proportions when it came to photos and memorabilia pertaining to her life, her career, her husbands and her children. She kept everything, including 110 huge scrapbooks, 20 hours of home movies, tons of documents, scripts, letters and personal effects of all sorts."

Among the items Lucie inherited from her mother in 1989 was an incredible and thorough collection of Lucille Ball's life. In that same interview, Lucie continued, "When we moved to New York I brought all the stuff with me. I donated some of it to Universal Studios and the Lucy Museum in Jamestown, New York, but I kept all the personal items." She kept the

Lucille Ball and Desi Arnaz *(AP Photo)*

scrapbooks knowing there was no way to display them so people could see all the wonderful things that were inside.

With the scrapbooks, Lucie produced a 1993 Emmy Award-winning documentary, *Lucy & Desi: A Home Movie.* Lucie stated, "In reality I only used a small portion from them because with a documentary you are dealing primarily with film footage and talking heads and then you throw in a few documents or letters or photos for texture."

Trying to shape a way to keep these memories, Lucie began digitizing the scrapbooks and placed that information onto a CD-ROM. Lucie's brother, Desi Arnaz, Jr., narrated and wrote and recorded the music for the CD. While the brother-and-sister team worked to preserve their mother's past, they came across tapes she had recorded, telling about her life. In an interview with *Collecting Online,* Desi stated, "It was really extraordinary to listen to the tapes my mother made, especially because we never knew they existed. They were just so very enlightening and interesting." Lucie continued, "It gave me an amazing feeling in the pit of my stomach. Like everyone, I walk into a room, turn on the television and *I Love Lucy* is on. That doesn't do the same thing to me as these tapes do. On the show that's Lucy Ricardo's voice. But when I heard my mother's voice on those tapes that really sounded like mom, it was very emotional for me. Sometimes I would laugh hysterically, and at other times it would be so sad."

They named the CD *Lucy & Desi: The Scrapbooks, Volume I: Made for Each Other.* With the CD, Lucy's lifelong collection will be preserved forever.

The late editor in chief and chairman of *Forbes* magazine, Malcolm Forbes, liked his toys. In his collection, there were approximately sixty thousand toy soldiers, whose illustrious service records included the Battle of Gettysburg, the Normandy Invasion, and the Battle of Waterloo. Malcolm Forbes spent twenty years accumulating the collection. Toy soldiers have probably been around as long as real soldiers, yet mass-produced toy soldiers only date to the 1890s.

Christie's in New York auctioned off part of this toy collection. The sale, which occurred in 1998, topped $1.4 million. Figures from the Forbes Museum of Military Miniatures, Tangier, brought bidding from around the world. Robert Forbes, president of Forbes Global Business and Finance, and son of Malcolm Forbes, stated, "We're absolutely thrilled with the results and with the fantastic experience we have had bringing our father's soldiers to new collectors through Christie's."

The top lot in the sale was a territorial battalion on active service in France, depicting the London Scottish, 13th Regiment, 56th London (Territorial) Division of 1915, with five battalion strength of five companies, which sold for $14,950. The grouping contained over six hundred pieces. Other highlights included an oil-on-canvas painting of a Dutch and British offshore sea battle, which fetched $5,175.

Even though the Tangier collection was sold off, the Forbes Gallery (at the Forbes Building in Manhattan) still has thousands of toy soldiers from Malcolm Forbes' collection on display. Located at 60 Fifth Avenue (corner of Twelfth Street) in New York City, the gallery is free and open to the public.

Forbes also collected Fabergé eggs. He began collecting in the 1930s, had one of the most advanced and exquisite collections of any collector, and allowed his collection to be viewed by the public. His collection was called the "Forbes Magazine Collection." Other collectors of Fabergé eggs include actress-comedienne Joan Rivers and her daughter, Melissa Rivers.

Malcolm Forbes
(AP Photo)

Tiny toy soldiers all march to the auction block at Christie's in a sale of the late Malcolm Forbes' prized toy collection. *(AP Photo)*

When you think of Vincent Price, the first thing that comes to mind is probably something on the scary side. With his acting and voice, Price had a way to put a scare into anybody. But there was more to Price than terror. The horror king's daughter, Victoria Price, talked about her father while promoting her book. She told of his collection of art and Native American pottery. In an interview with *USA Today*, Price talked of her father's softer side as an urbane art lover. He had a love for many styles of Native American art and pottery work produced by Native Americans.

Vincent Price *(AP Photo)*

A pair of fifty-year-old antique skeleton chairs once part of a dining room collection owned by Vincent Price. *(AP Photo)*

Frank Sinatra was the legendary performer with a voice like no other. I remember when Sinatra was traveling the country in the 1980s, on tour with Sammy Davis, Jr., and Dean Martin. I was one of the first standing in line to snap up tickets to the show. Sure, the majority of the people in line around me were much older, but I knew this was an opportunity to witness history. This was an opportunity to see a renowned entertainer whom I might never be able to see again. It was certainly worth every minute.

Frank "Ol' Blue Eyes" Sinatra was known as an actor and singer. He was also a train collector and an avid one. His home in Palm Springs was filled with the miniature versions of the locomotives Sinatra remembered, as well as the color orange. Sinatra had said, "Orange is the happiest color," and he truly was happy living at his desert home. Sinatra sang in public for the last time on Saturday, February 25, 1995. Shortly thereafter, the Sinatras put the home on the market so Frank could take up full-time residence in Malibu and Beverly Hills. Canadian businessman Jim Pattison now owns the compound. The house was sold complete with furnishings and Sinatra's train sets. It was difficult for Sinatra to leave, and he stayed on as a guest for a few months after the sale, only leaving after one of Pattison's representatives moved onto the property. "I think leaving that house and all the things he loved there was one of the hardest things he ever had to do," stated a representative for Pattison. It was reported that leaving the house was a devastation from which Sinatra never recovered. He passed away three years later in Los Angeles on May 14, 1998.

Sinatra was gone, but his memories remain throughout the house. The projection room has a gathering of black-and-white photos of Sinatra from his various films. Sinatra was an avid art collector, and the home is still filled with bright and colorful pieces. A voracious reader, Sinatra would sit in the Kennedy Room and read books from the collection for hours.

The singer and actor was most productive in the '50s and '60s, belting out tunes and acting in a variety of films. Between work, Sinatra would retreat to his desert home to relax and enjoy. There, he would spend hours in his Train Room. The room held a miniature replica of his hometown of Hoboken, New Jersey. According to a story in *Architectural Digest,* designer Bea Korshak stated, "Frank had always collected trains. He would climb up there and move things around. It's nosier than a real station when everything is running."

Sinatra's splendid Lionel O-gauge layout and collection was specifically constructed. It was twelve feet by twenty-four feet, and the layout was based on Lionel's 1949 New York showroom layout. The rheostat-controlled, incandescent lights of the trains can simulate early morning, noontime, and evening lighting. In the 1980s Sinatra built a reproduction of the Lionel no. 2787 freight station after seeing a photo of it in a Lionel catalog. According to a story in *Classic Toy Trains,* the collection is large and diverse. From prewar Lionel to modern Lionel and LGB, toy trains in many sizes and from many manufacturers lined the walls. Sinatra was not satisfied with one make or model; he loved all types of trains, including

European models by Marklin and Hornby. According to *Classic Toy Trains,* the most unusual piece in his collection was an Italian wooden train, made by the Elina Company in Italy during the 1850s and 1860s. The train was a gift from the Vatican. Sinatra's collection included train memorabilia as well, with photographs of steam engines and framed paintings gracing the walls.

The collection is laid out on oak cabinets with glass shelves. Included is an underground passenger station, where commuter cars stop to pick up passengers; an agriculture area with grain elevators; and an early 1960s Lionel presidential passenger set. In one area, cars pass through a freight yard. Another section, where Sinatra once had a winter scene, is decorated for Christmas. Sinatra even had his train building patterned after a freight station.

Pattison intends to keep the collection together, both for the importance of the collection and the significance of it being such an important part of Sinatra's life.

Sinatra's songs, ways, and life were unquestionably his own throughout his eighty-two years. Making no apologies, he was his own man and succeeded in television, films, and recordings. He was an avid collector who loved his hobby, his family, and what he did in life.

DID YOU KNOW?

Frank Sinatra Jr. is a collector himself. He told me he collects miniature lighthouses. "I have several of them. Most of them I have ordered from catalogs. They are very unique and intricate." Sinatra was nice enough to sign a miniature lighthouse for a Cystic Fibrosis auction. The piece, with a copy of *Greetings with Love: The Book of Valentines* signed by the author and Sinatra, sold for $650.

Opposite: Frank Sinatra *(AP Photo)*

These amazing trains were part of Frank's collection, which he housed in his Palm Springs home. *(Courtesy Classic Toy Trains and Jim Pattison)*

LUCILLE BALL

The impact Lucille Ball made on the collecting world is great. That bright-red hair can be found on many Lucy look-a-like dolls produced over the years. Lucy collectibles number in the thousands. Most are relatively inexpensive, while items dating back to the show *I Love Lucy* are more rare and therefore higher in price. Some celebrities gain in popularity after their death; Lucille Ball was popular in life and has continued to keep people smiling, even after her death. She is a true icon.

Lucy can still appear on screen with this collectible.

Lucille Ball salt and pepper shakers

Some of the stars who have been re-created in doll form include Brandy Norwood, Lucille Ball, Elizabeth Taylor, Audrey Hepburn, Rosie O'Donnell, Elvis Presley, Kate Winslet, Britney Spears, and Shirley Temple. And that's just the tip of the iceberg. In fact, I wrote an entire book, *Buying and Selling Celebrity Dolls,* on the subject, and it included a listing of over five thousand celebrity dolls. Celebrity-inspired collectibles are a multimillion-dollar business.

Luke Skywalker and Princess Leia dolls are very collectible today.

Dolls of the cast of *Welcome Back, Kotter.*

Dolls from past television shows are popular with collectors.

With the tragic death of Princess Diana, the increase in collectibles bearing her image has skyrocketed. Everything from stamps to dolls to porcelain dishes has been made in her likeness. The "people's princess" was into helping others, and many times, the company offering the collectible item promises that a portion of the sale's proceeds will be donated to one of Diana's charities. Collectible magazine covers are easily accessible since several tribute issues have been released since Diana's death, and the cost to the collector is low in most instances. Autographed photos of the princess sell for close to two thousand dollars today. Her signature on a card can go from one hundred dollars to five hundred dollars.

Diana collectibles are some of the hottest on the market. Even Ty, with the Beanie Babies, got into the Diana explosion, issuing a Princess Beanie Baby. The purple bear is marked with a pastel rose over its heart. Ty stated that all its profits from Princess Beanie would go to the Diana, Princess of Wales Memorial Fund.

Dolls are another big category of Diana collectibles. Many companies have produced Princess Diana dolls, ranging in price from a few dollars to thousands of dollars. Older dolls are highly in demand. Well-known companies, such as the Danbury Mint, the Franklin Mint, and Ashton-Drake Galleries, made many of the dolls produced.

Clothing worn by the late princess is also highly sought after. One gown alone sold for over $220,000. Diana even has a stamp made in her likeness. The tragedy of her death was enormous. She was a much-loved figure who will remain in our memories for years to come, partly because of her work and smiling face, partly because of the collectibles now made in her honor.

A Diana Plate commemorating the life of Diana, Princess of Wales

A Princess Diana-inspired Beanie Baby and a biography on the princess are among collector's items that will be strong sellers for years to come.

I love Marilyn Monroe. I was only a toddler when she died, but her impact on me, as well as on the millions of other Americans across the country, is nothing short of astounding. It would have been nice if Monroe had been a collector, but she was not. Despite her fame and fortune, Monroe lived a very simple life. Born Norma Jean Baker on June 1, 1926, the beautiful star left this earth in 1962 at the age of thirty-six. She loved the music of Frank Sinatra, TWA was her favorite airline, and her favorite actors included Marlon Brando, Clark Gable, Greta Garbo, and Jean Harlow. Her only extravagances were shopping at Bloomingdale's and drinking Dom Perignon 1953. She wasn't one to hold on to many things, except, perhaps, dreams.

Her persona today has not been shadowed, evident in the mass amounts of Marilyn Monroe memorabilia available. Magazine covers include everything from her first appearance on *Family Circle* to her well-known picture gracing the cover of the inaugural issue of *Playboy.* Other Monroe collectibles include Barbie dolls made in her likeness, plates, mugs, figures, pillows, perfume bottles, cigarette lighters, and over one hundred books written about her. Almost every type of item that is made has had a Marilyn image on it. You can even pick up a bottle of wine—perhaps, a bottle of Marilyn Merlot or a commemorative whiskey bottle with Marilyn in her famous skirt-blowing pose for a mere $350.

Because of her marriage to baseball great Joe DiMaggio, memorabilia related to DiMaggio began to soar and has been a hot item ever since.

Today, Marilyn Monroe collectibles are hotter than ever. A Marilyn Monroe doll made in 1997 by Mattel sells for around sixty dollars. A plate with her image by the Bradford Exchange can cost around thirty-five dollars, or you can pick up her autograph from anywhere between fifteen hundred and five thousand dollars. One of the most desirable pieces of Monroe memorabilia, besides articles that once belonged to her or were worn by her, is the first issue of *Playboy* magazine, with Marilyn on the cover and a nude pictorial inside. That magazine, which originally sold for fifty cents, retails in the $750 range today. The price varies depending on condition. Marilyn is now an icon in the world of collecting. Try as you might, you still may never be able to get hold of everything with her image on it. One thing is for sure; it would be a lot of fun trying.

Marilyn Monroe *(AP Photo)*

One of Marilyn Monroe's dresses, sold at a Christie's auction.

The King of Rock-'n'-Roll, Elvis Presley was both a collector and the person with whom collectors can relate. Presley starred in thirty-three films, made history with his television appearances, and sold over one billion records globally, more than any other artist. His American sales have earned him gold, platinum, or multiplatinum awards for 140 different albums and singles. His talent, good looks, and charisma attracted many to his records and items bearing his image.

Elvis memorabilia was always popular, but after his death at his Memphis home, Graceland, on August 16, 1977, Elvis memorabilia began to explode. Vintage Elvis merchandise, including old records, autographs, concert tickets, photographs, and movie posters, is highly sought after and not as easily accessible as the newer mass-produced items. An Elvis signature can run in the thousands of dollars. Graceland's own archives department even acquires such memorabilia at times, adding to their already large collection. On average, there are over six thousand listings on eBay under the search word "Elvis." The highest-priced item at the time of this writing was a ten-thousand-square-foot repli-ca, located in Los Angeles, of Elvis Presley's Graceland. The starting price was $7,500,000, which included over $1,200,000 worth of vintage Elvis artifacts, including gold records and a guitar. The least expensive items offered were Elvis movie stills, starting at one cent.

Top: Elvis Presley with his wife, Priscilla, and daughter, Lisa Marie. *(Courtesy Shooting Stars)*

Collectible Elvis Presley album covers and an Elvis-inspired doll and guitar.

ROY ROGERS

Roy Rogers was one of the most loved cowboys ever to grace the screen. When he passed away in 1998, his legacy was protected by not only his film career, but also by a thirty-three-thousand square-foot museum, originally in Victorville, California, and now in Branson, Missouri. The museum is a testimony of Rogers' love for collecting. Rogers, whose real name was Leonard Slye, appeared in over ninety movies after moving to California in the 1930s. He got his film start with Republic Pictures, which was just beginning a search for a new singing cowboy. The producer picked Rogers and the rest is history. In 1947, Rogers met Dale Evans, and they were soon married.

Rogers told *Collecting* magazine, "When I was a kid, we didn't have camera. If you look in the museum, you'll see only one or two little pictures of me when I was about 3 and 5 years old." He continued talking about his collection, "We have old Trigger in there like he was. We had him physically mounted, rearing on his hind legs. It's hard for me to stand there and look at him. He was such a great part of my life because nobody thought of Roy Rogers without Trigger. I made my first picture with him, I made my last picture with him, and I made my TV series with him. He was 33 when he passed away. That's like a person at 115."

Rogers stated that he had planned on leaving his collection of memorabilia to his children. He told *Collecting,* "I only have one life. I've been thinking about this for years because of all the children who grew up with me. I'm going to leave my collection to the kids, and whatever they want to do with it is OK with me." Fortunately, that memorabilia has been preserved for collectors and Roy Rogers lovers for years to come in the Roy Rogers Museum. Many Roy Rogers collectibles, including vintage posters, plates, dolls, lunch boxes, paper collectibles, and more are available today. Happy trails to you . . . until we meet again.

Roy Rogers with Dale Evans *(Courtesy the Roy Rogers Museum)*

Roy Rogers comic *(Courtesy the Roy Rogers Museum)*

Frank Sinatra collectibles are very strong in the marketplace. The singer recorded more than one hundred albums and earned nine Grammy awards. Music collectors are interested generally in the older music rather than the format, seventy-eights from the 1940s and 1950s. Most can be purchased for less than ten dollars, with the exception of Sinatra's first recording. He was a vocalist on "From the Bottom of My Heart," a 1939 recording by Harry James and his orchestra. A copy, in excellent condition, sells for five hundred to seven hundred dollars. A Christmas recording of a four-record set in seven-inch extended-play format from 1950, titled *Christmas Songs by Sinatra,* can run $150 in excellent condition.

Since Sinatra's death, a multitude of memorabilia items have hit the market, including dolls, cups, clocks, ties, and plates. Just about anything that can be made with his likeness has been. Though mass marketed and in some ways exploitative, this keeps his image alive for those who knew his work and those yet to experience his golden voice.

Collectible Sinatra albums bring the voice of the famous crooner into your home.

Buffalo Bob, creator of the lovable Howdy Doody, influenced a generation of children from 1947 until 1960. The original Howdy Doody was seen in over twenty-five hundred episodes of the *Howdy Doody Show*. Smith had said, "The original Howdy Doody would probably sell for $1." However, the original Howdy Doody marionette sold for $23,000 at a Christie's East auction in 1995. In the early 1950s, you could buy a Howdy Doody marionette toy for about $3.49. That toy today is worth around $450 in the box. The Flub-a-Dub marionette, which sold for $2.98, now commands upwards of $1,500 due to its rarity. The words "It's Howdy Doody Time" have been scrawled across T-shirts, watches, coloring books, and even fudge bars.

Buffalo Bob Smith was born in 1917. His real name is Robert Schmidt, but everyone knows him as Bob. He started professionally in radio at the age of fifteen and worked as a singer and musician, playing the piano. In 1947, NBC was looking for someone to do a live children's show on television. The one-hour program was a big hit. Many characters came about as the show continued, including Princess Winterspring Summerfall, Clarabell, Phineas T. Bluster, Chief Thunderthud, Dilly Dally, and Flub-a-Dub. Merchandising mania followed, and today items from the show are highly collectible.

Smith told *Collecting* magazine, "Many times people ask me what my most memorable moment was doing the *Howdy Doody Show*. Well, I say, we had many firsts. [We were] the first show on television [each day]. There was the test pattern all day long until 5:30 P.M. when I would come on and say, 'Hey, kids! What time is it?' We were the first show in color and the first show with live music. But the biggest thrill was 10 years after Howdy went off the air! We were on from '47-'60. Then in 1970, I was invited to the University of Pennsylvania to do a show for the graduate students. I thought they were putting me on! This fellow said, 'No! We want you to come, wear a costume—in short we want to relive our happy, carefree childhood days.'"

The nostalgia of Howdy Doody and Buffalo Bob Smith will never really ever go away. The time will also always be right for collecting their memorabilia. Any time is Howdy Doody time.

Buffalo Bob Smith and Howdy Doody

Howdy Doody waves hello.

It was lots of fun talking to different celebrities, even if they weren't collectors. Though I have to say, the majority of them did collect.

Katie Couric told me, "No, I'm not really a collector." But she does have a great collection of fans who watch her each morning. Katie is pictured with my husband, Joe, and I.

We didn't get a chance to go golfing with Richard Karn, but we had a chance to chat about collecting!

Chuck Berry said, "Sorry, sweetie, I'm not a collector!"

Rodney Dangerfield before his death told me, "Michele, I don't collect anything *except jokes!*"

Lou Ferrigno and I at a collectors' show.

George Hamilton, a fun guy and a big collector. We got together in Florida on a nice, sunny day.

Can you believe that with the amount of access to rock-'n'-roll and music personalities and memorabilia he has, Casey Kasem is not a collector? "Sorry Michele, I just don't collect anything." Maybe we can change that with some prodding.

Frankie Avalon should probably collect 1950s memorabilia. But he told me he doesn't collect anything.

Actress Jayne Meadows told me, "I don't collect anything. Never have. Except for friends. How do I stop is the big question! I've been collecting them since childhood."

Rush Limbaugh in Seattle with my husband, Joe, and I at a party of his.

Actor Bill Murray told me he really doesn't collect anything, but he does love anything to do with baseball. When I offered him a book I had on the history of baseball, he replied, "Yes! I'd love to have that!" He is one of the funniest guys I've ever met.

Jay North of *Dennis the Menace* fame caught up with me in Florida. He doesn't collect much, but he does have some memorabilia from the show.

Television-show host Wink Martindale is a collector. He likes several things—especially bright-colored jackets! Pictured with my husband, Joe, and I, Wink told me he also collects records.

Butch Patrick (Eddie Munster) says, "I collect hats—lots of them!"